JOURNEYS
ON THE
RAZOR-EDGED
PATH

SIMONS ROOF

ILLUSTRATIONS BY FRANK KRAMER

THOMAS Y. CROWELL COMPANY

NEW YORK · ESTABLISHED 1834

TO MY FATHER AND MOTHER

WALTER AND LILA ROOF

WHOSE LOVE TAUGHT ME HIS

AUTHOR'S NOTE

This book may seem at first glance to cover a rather odd assortment of subjects, ranging from a grass-eating tiger, Dhruva and the white ants, and a bull and a kitten, to spiritual transmutation, meditation, and *sadhana;* from Indian yogis, Tibetan lamas, and people in the Kalimpong bazaar, to poverty, fasts, alcohol, and sex; and from psychic powers, stories of holy men, and gurus and chelas, to the Ear-Whispered Doctrine, animism and monotheism, and a Mountain God. But they all, first and last, are about inner and outer journeys on the razor-edged path, and they attempt to reveal the changes in consciousness which occur in the quest of God.

The setting is the Himalayas, and the town is Kalimpong, where we have lived the majority of our twenty-six months in India. Kalimpong is in the Darjeeling District, in a pocket of India close to Tibet, Nepal, Pakistan, Sikkim, and Bhutan. From Kalimpong, which is the major center for trade with

Tibet, we can reach the border of any of these five countries in less than a day of travel. But there is more about Kalimpong and its people in these pages—and more too about the snowy crests around us which jut up from Tibet, Nepal, Sikkim, and India, and more about Kanchenjunga and its shining place in our sky. And, because "the path with an edge like a razor's" follows the heart rather than physical geography, I have let it wind its way, sometimes to places as distant as a ship in the South Seas and a cathedral on a St. Nicholas' Day in Naples.

The book has grown out of the comparative (and contrastive) studies in religion which have been my sole pursuit in India. The stories, of which there are many, are of my own making unless otherwise noted. Of the stories of Indian origin, I have favored to some extent those told or retold by Sri Ramakrishna (the nineteenth-century saint of India who was also one of its master storytellers).

Finally, my indebtedness for help and encouragement is heavy, and beyond full acknowledgment. There are the friends whose warm interest and inspiration have been ever-present. And there are numerous others: swamis of the Ramakrishna order who gave constant gracious assistance; Christian ministers and priests; Buddhist lamas and monks; Muslim mullahs and scholars; Hindu sadhus of many philosophies and cults; and friends of many other religions, from Jains and Sikhs to Parsis and Shintoists. And there is the countless number of Indians, Tibetans, Sikkimese, Nepalese, Pakistanis, Bhutanese, and others we met, who made us feel at home and as one with them. To all of these I give my deepest thanks, in the name of the Father of us all.

CONTENTS

JOURNEYS ON THE RAZOR-EDGED PATH

1. SOME APPROACHES TO THE RAZOR'S EDGE

I.   A TALE OF THE SUFFICIENT CAUSE

Near a small town in the Himalayas, there once lived a beloved old *sadhu* [1] whose saintly life had inspired many to seek him as a teacher. He had always declined to have pupils, since his path had been other than that of a spiritual preceptor. But one day, believing he must now begin to "replace" himself in the world against the time of his departure from it, he agreed with a younger sadhu to accept a small

---

[1] *Sadhu* (pronounced "sod-who")—a "holy man."

I

number of pupils. The elated young man rushed off and soon returned with nine men of widely varied ages.

"Sir," he announced happily, "here is the first group of applicants for you to interview."

"Let them come in one by one," the old sadhu directed.

And to each in turn he asked but a single question. "Why do you wish to undertake the strenuous disciplines of the spiritual life?"

The oldest applicant, who entered first, replied: "I have tasted every fruit of the world—from the love of beautiful women and the power of money to a degree of popularity and even a little fame—and I have only memories to show for it, which time and a small wisdom have turned sour."

The next man, a forester, exclaimed: "There is a Mighty Presence in the woods where I walk! There is a miracle wherever I look—in the poorest little pebble, the least little flower, the strangest little insect. And then, the trees, the rivers, the mountains—and, O sir, the stars! Tell me how to meet Him!"

Another, a shop owner, whispered: "Twice in this month have I known tragedy. My young wife died in childbirth. Then, only yesterday, my infant son himself. Give me the peace of God if you can, or I will give myself the peace of death."

A perplexed temple attendant explained: "In my temple we honor a certain God. In other temples honor is given to other Gods. And I think of all the Gods of all the other religions. Which among these, sir, is the greatest and the true God?"

The next, a student, declared: "God blesses most those who serve Him best. Since I will prosper according to how

I serve Him, I wish to know the innermost secrets of pleasing Him."

A poor farmer said: "I am afraid—very afraid. My family is large. Even in good times I can scarcely feed all the mouths. What would happen if I became very sick or if I died? Teach me how to win God's help, I beg you!"

Another, a scholar, sighed: "So many books, all disproving each other . . . Reason forces me to conclude that either there is something higher than reason or there is nothing sensible about life at all."

A middle-aged clerk complained: "I live in hell itself! My wife's tongue drips poison for me. My children continually whine and beg after me. My employer despises me and threatens every day to discharge me. I have begun to hate everybody and I no longer know what to do with myself."

The last, a boy of sixteen, said shyly: "I am not worthy to be taught, sir. But I could do errands and fetch firewood and water and do the cleaning up. And if it would not offend you, sir, while you were teaching the others I would sometimes listen if my work were nearby."

While the applicants waited outside, the old sadhu spoke softly to his friend. "How many reasons they have—satiety, wonder, suffering, ignorance, ambition, fear, logic, frustration, and love. Which of these reasons," he asked, "do you find most acceptable—and which applicants would you favor?"

The young man started to reply, then lapsed into a long thoughtful silence. Once more he began to speak, but again fell silent.

"Bring them all in," the old sadhu said, smiling. "This will be our group. For the reason of any one of them is as good as the reason of any other. Any cause for turning to God is sufficient."

2. YOU DON'T HAVE TO BELIEVE IN GOD TO BEGIN

You don't have to believe in God to begin the practice of spiritual disciplines. . . . Even after several thousand years of the declaration of this simple fact by spiritual teachers of every religion, its utterance still comes as a colossal shock to many people. And the second half of this statement, which seems to be equally unrealized by most persons, is similarly startling. . . . *But if you persist in the right practice of spiritual disciplines, you will inevitably not only believe in God but you will experience the One Reality.*

Belief about God is one thing, knowing God is another. Belief is subject to limited or misleading information and doubt, but knowing from personal experience is not. How, spiritual teachers ask, can a newcomer to the religious life be expected to know what is knowable only through direct God-realization?

The timeless contention of spiritual teachers is this. There are tested methods of developing one's vast innate potentialities—of releasing finer character qualities and greater abilities. Even a few weeks or months of proper experimentation is enough to convince most normally intelligent people of this fact. The disciplines include meditation—the mastery of emotions and mind; study—familiarization with one's own constitution and the laws of the spiritual life; and service—how to exact the most productive results from every expenditure of thought and energy.

By following these disciplines, the teachers promise, you will soon discover that your most extraordinary inherent capacities are of a spiritual nature, and that true greatness of being is potential within you. And as you learn to utilize these newfound capacities, they say, eventually you will attain those states of consciousness in which you will directly *experience*, in fullest awareness and beyond all possible doubt, the incommunicable knowledge of God.

3. RUNNING A RACE THAT NEVER BEGAN

At one time I knew a man in his eighties who, for most of his years, had been preparing to lead "a great spiritual life." He had a home like a religious factory, geared to produce at the least, you would think, a major saint or a minor god. He had a magnificent prayer room, decorated with the symbols of his four favorite religions—and space left for the symbolism of a fifth faith which would unify the other four, he declared, and to which he meant some day to give his "dedicated thought." He had collected religious art objects, many of them lovely and rare, from all over the world, and he would discuss their significance with you; but first he would tell you how he had acquired certain pieces at prices which were "actually sinfully low." He had a mahogany-walled library with thousands of religious books he had carefully catalogued, and he worked quite hard, from time to time, on a schedule of how his "special studies" should begin.

He had a list, which he modestly showed his friends, of a dozen or so "tentative social service projects," and usually on rainy days and days when he felt mildly indisposed, he said, he hastened the final revision of his plans. He addressed a heavy correspondence to ministers, priests, and sadhus, although he confessed to me, in a voice of gentle complaint, their own replies were, on the whole, "almost discourteously light." . . . And so, with all that he spent, he never invested enough in himself; and he failed to do the simple thing that might have helped. Wandering through his splendid spiritual factory, so lavishly equipped to make him great, he never had the time for one little task: to touch the starting switch.

4. THE NEED TO RECOGNIZE RATHER THAN TO ACQUIRE

To a youth who was sadly reciting his inadequacy to begin spiritual disciplines, a *guru* [2] made the following reply:

"You are like a man who, unknown to himself, sits above a diamond mine while bemoaning his poverty; and in the mine is represented your physical potentiality.

"You are like a man who, possessing a fine ship with which he might sail all the seas of the world, worries over the fickleness of weather and water instead of mastering his ship; and in the ship is represented your emotional potentiality.

"You are like a man who, owning a library which contains the secrets of human knowledge, is too involved with the trivialities of the moment to learn the difficult language

[2] *Guru* (pronounced "goo-roo")—a spiritual teacher.

of the books of wisdom; and in the library is represented your mental potentiality.

"You are like a man who, unaware that he is the inheritor of the greatest of all kingdoms, lives the life of a beggar; and in the kingdom is represented your spiritual potentiality.

"You possess all you need. There is nothing to acquire. You have only to learn to recognize what is already yours.

"Hold up your head. Lift up your heart. Claim your priceless inheritance!"

5. THE GRASS-EATING TIGER

A tigress was attacking a herd of goats, an old Indian parable goes, when she gave birth to a cub and died. The cub grew up among the goats, so that all it ever knew were goat ways. It ate grass like a goat and it bleated like a goat. And one day, when it was grown and a big tiger came to attack the herd, the grass-eating tiger was terrified. When the goats bleated in terror and ran away, so did the grass-eating tiger. But the other tiger, dumbfounded to see such a strange fellow creature, bounded after it and soon caught it. While the grass-eating tiger set up a fearful bleating, and tried unsuccessfully to butt its head against its captor, the other tiger dragged it to a pool and made it stare at their reflection in the water. "See!" the big tiger commanded. "You are just like me!" Then, after a short hunt, it gave the grass-eating tiger some meat to eat. And while the grass-eating tiger chewed it with relish, marveling that it could ever have been contented with grass, the other tiger exclaimed softly: "Ah, now you begin to see there is no difference between us! Come—follow me in the life to which you belong."

So, the sages of India say, you should attend only to those who know who you are and what your true nature is. Be not misled into believing yourself a goat when you are truly a tiger.

6. ON THE WAY

I remember the morning when I was on the final ascent to Kalimpong. I was talking with an orange-robed young monk, also headed for the Himalayas, about what the mountains might have in store for us.

And I was thinking how, at some time, probably each of us has a dream of a place that sustains us, that somewhere awaits us, if only we could find it, a forgotten fragment of Paradise. How for some it is a hidden valley, where time rests and every day is eternity; for some a lovely island, floating like a flower on a sunlit sea; and for some a place of sacred solitude, where the golden air seems to whisper echoes from the voice of God.

"This is what I have always wanted," I said slowly, pointing to the great mountains before us. "Every man, I think, has a mountain to climb; something has told me to seek here for mine."

He faced me, smiling seriously. "Yes, in the Himalayas," he replied, with faith-filled eyes, "it is said that all who earnestly seek, find. So many, for thousands of years, have come here—to be closer to God. And now may you find your mountain, and I"—his words were a happy prayer—"may I, if it pleases God, find mine."

He turned then, and I with him, to gaze at the mountains, at the snow-lit fields of silence ahead.

7. A REASON FOR SELF-FULFILLMENT

A man I know says his reason for wanting to test the efficacy of spiritual disciplines is frankly selfish—he wants to perfect himself. He believes that the reasons why many people come to the religious life are equally selfish; that many accept at face value Jesus' promise that "What things soever ye desire, when ye pray, believe that ye receive them, and ye shall have them," and he believes this kind of prayer practice must have an equivalent in every religion. And so, he contends, many of those who first look to God do so out of desire. They want something: food, shelter, money, power, pleasant work, greater talent, recovery from illness, escape from fear, "Undo, O Lord, what I've done," "Please don't let the inevitable happen," "Give me rush service, dear Saviour, on this one little miracle—"

It is wise for us, certainly, not to be burdened with illusions as to why many people initially search for God. The reasons he cites, as far as they go, sound familiar; and we should remember that, sadly, many people never move beyond the stage of fascination with miracles.

One morning, for instance, I had a caller who wanted to sell an old Tibetan manuscript. "This a very strong magic book—" he said persuasively, "*very* holy! How to call out the rain. How to make the hailstorm bang up your enemies' crops. How to punish the wicked—break legs or necks." I asked why he wished to sell this awesome document. "Lama say I no good man to make the magic," he explained, with candid humor. "Maybe you do it. You swear you not make the magic in Kalimpong, I sell, *very* cheap!" I swore I wouldn't make the magic anywhere, and declined. And once I had a letter from a young Nigerian (who knew of me through a mutual friend), beseeching me to explain all I might know of "how to get good fast prayer reply from Master God." He explained his request in a conscience-stricken postscript. He had got a girl with child and wanted Master God to "hurry fix things up different" (the girl wasn't pregnant after all, he later wrote, but had been trying to force him into marriage—which, he wrote still later, he had agreed to since she loved him *that* much). I also recall a politician who joined our church when I was a youngster. By diligent work for several years and much public prayer that he might become "a fit instrument of our Lord," he succeeded in being elected president of the congregation, was appointed on his church-built reputation to a high political office, then quickly drifted away from religion because he had won what he wanted.

But we also have to acknowledge the many who are exceptions. And these are the individuals who generally seek not just the usual surface practices of religion, but who go deeper, who earnestly adopt a disciplined life of meditation, study, and service, who know how to forget self and to work for others.

This is true of one of my friends who witnessed a child's death by starvation during a famine in West Bengal and who says she heard, more real than any sound before or since, a voice clearly telling her to serve His poor. Another friend turned this way because he believes that a last-second prayer for help, after his ship had been torpedoed and he was wounded and drowning, caused his miraculous rescue. Still another found his reason during a moment of enlightenment when, staring at a little violet with its blossom just free of a fresh snowfall, he experienced simultaneously the whole harmonious play of the seasons and the sense of a Supreme Life cyclically manifesting itself through all the transient forms of existence. Another reports that, while listening out of curiosity to a swami [3] lecture on Christianity to a Boston audience, he suddenly perceived for the first time what Christianity could mean to him, and was inspired, from that moment, to seek the total transformation of his life. And another, deeply moved by the quiet poise and compassion of a friend at the scene of a tragic automobile accident, sought from the friend the secret of his serenity and discovered meditation and, through it, discovered himself.

Any first reason for seeking God will do; but not every first reason can sustain one. Our greatest latent capacities occur at the spiritual level, and only at that level can they be released in the personality. To seek personality integration is satisfactory as an immediate goal, but a better aspiration is to dedicate oneself to achieving a soul-infused self. It helps tremendously, though it is not necessary, if there is recognition from the start that the search for self-realization is identical with the quest of God-realization. And this means that one should act on the basic premise that only the

[3] Swami—a title of respect, comparable to the Christian "Reverend" or "Father," properly applied only to qualified graduates of Hindu monastic training.

pure in heart can know God. An ancient statement to ponder in connection with this is that "You can have anything you want as long as you do not want it for yourself."

If we want "good fast prayer reply from Master God," we need to study, if we will, the identity of selflessness and love and the identity of selfishness and hate; we need to accept the time-worn evidence that selflessness and love offer more to humanity—to us—than selfishness and hate; and, if we are willing, to resolve to point our lives toward the wise service of others. As a start let our guide be to seek self-fulfillment with intelligent love, in order to be of greater service to others. To work for true self-perfection involves the systematic and healthy development of one's totality of being; and the single key—there is no other—is to learn to utilize the full resources of the spiritual self. Paradoxically, you can have only what you are willing to give away. The saint's love is like a river perpetually flowing into the sea.

8.   HOW TO BE SOUGHT AFTER

"But why try to find God?" a critic asked his minister.

"You don't have to," the minister replied gently. "If you can get yourself out of mind God will find you."

9.   THE MOTIVE OF LOVE

Why begin to tread the razor's edge? Why begin the difficult disciplines of the spiritual life? Beyond your immediate and personal reason, what enduring motive is there to sustain the effort? You will discover many new incentives as you proceed: a joy and a peace which are unknown outside of the spiritual way; the quiet excitement of developing your best qualities and abilities; an inspiring sense of power for good as you attain the steady strength of true self-control; the development of compassion and its rich fulfillment in relieving the sufferings of others; the capacity to work always from the inmost calm center of being, to be the same person, at all times, in all circumstances; and many more incentives, each leading to the next and a better. But ultimately it seems to me, after we have exhausted a series of increasingly worthy motives wrought out of the pain and pleasure of experience, we reach that point beyond which even the saints have not been able to venture. And then, like them, we are content to describe our motive in a few simple words: *through love to know God and to do His will.*

2. DOUBT AND THE WAY
OF KNOWLEDGE

I. DON'T LOOK FOR TRUTH IN THE WRONG DIRECTION

"We should never doubt the divine value of an honest doubt," the swami said quietly.

High up the mountain, in a lovely little garden carved like a bowl out of the gray rock, we sat and talked, sipping the fragrant tangy tea which is locally grown. Sometimes we gazed at the ledge partly overhanging the garden, from which long sprays of white orchids, with bright yellow centers, cascaded almost to our feet. Sometimes we looked below us at Kalimpong, sprawling over the saddle between two mountains, its homes scattered out casually from the crowded bazaar, and merging quickly with the tiny Nepalese farms and their terraced fields of paddy. Sometimes, as we do habitually in these parts, we turned toward the great jagged wall of snow that blocks a long side of our sky, and then, momentarily silent, we brooded on the radiant crest of Kanchenjunga itself, filling our hearts through our eyes. And we looked at each other, a group representing many religions, and talked less of our differences and more of our similarities. But the youth who had come with the swami now began to worry about the differences.

"But see, sir," the boy protested earnestly, "all of you believe such different things. Surely somebody is wrong! And look down there—" he said more passionately, pointing towards the town, "temples for Hindus, lamaseries for Buddhists, a mosque for Muslims, a church for Christians! Out of all these ways—and more—how can an honest person know where to begin? How, that is," he added more soberly, "can *I* know where to begin?"

The swami glanced around the sympathetic group. And then, at his unspoken invitation, a few pointed with a slight gesture toward the youth and others nodded toward him in agreement.

Turning to the somewhat baffled-looking young man, the swami spoke kindly: "They are telling you, these gentlemen of many different religions, that you are looking for truth in the wrong direction. They would suggest, I believe, that you use your doubt wisely. And so they would have you remember, my son, that truth can be found nowhere except in a man's own soul. The true path for you to follow, then, is the path that leads within."

Slowly the boy began to smile.

"Do you disagree with such an approach?" the swami asked.

"I doubt it," he grinned.

2.   BOOK KNOWLEDGE, AUTHORITY, AND EXPERIENCE

The subtlest danger in spiritual learning is to substitute faith in book knowledge, or blind faith in authority, for direct experience. This is so in both West and East, where many religiously minded people confuse an emotional-devotional attachment or an intellectual attitude with an experiential belief.

The place above all where we have to be absolutely honest about what we know and what we do not know is spiritual knowledge. We must have discrimination enough to recognize what we unmistakably know, and integrity enough to question what we only surmise may be true. On one hand are the facts of our own experience; on the other, the hypotheses suggested to us by others. And a hypothesis is of value only as we experiment to determine whether it has validity for us.

One of the gravest dangers of organized religion lies in the tendency to ask the devotee simply to accept a creed or dogma rather than to insist that he investigate it diligently in his own life through meditation, study, and service.

Is the Christ the Son of God? How can you know the answer beyond all doubt? This is not a proposition to be accepted because you have read it and heard it many times. It is not to be accepted on authority—there are many authorities making claims for many gods. It is not to be accepted even on the basis of your own reasoning, because spiritual truth is intuitively perceived in a realm which transcends the limitations of the everyday mind. Instead it is essentially a matter for individual investigation; for contemplating and testing in one's own life; and for affirming through direct realization of its truth in higher consciousness. The difference between the aspirant and the disciple is that the aspirant says I believe, and the disciple, I know.

If we now believe, what then but to *know?*

3. ON THE IMPORTANCE OF UNBELIEF

One morning a friend of mine stopped by a *gompa* [1] and asked to see a learned and likable but somewhat opinionated young monk. But the elderly lama he inquired of shook his head dubiously. "He's meditating, and I'm afraid he's going to be a very long time. You see," he explained, with a faint hint of a smile, "the abbot just told him he knows so much that now he's got to start to unbelieve it."

4. THE TRUTH SEEKER

The truth seeker,
after years of search,
met a smiling old sage
seated in a mountain cave.
Books were everywhere.
"These," the sage explained,
"are the secret volumes
which contain the sum
of all human wisdom.
Each seeker may have one;

[1] *Gompa*—the Tibetan word commonly used in the Kalimpong area to designate a Buddhist monastery.

which do you wish?"
And the truthseeker,
surveying how endless
the number of them seemed,
at last replied slowly:
"Only that book, sir,
which can teach me all
that the others contain."
"Such a book exists,"
the sage said; and then,
smiling with a wise sadness,
handed the truth seeker
"The Book of Doubt."

5. WHY THE DRAGON IS REALLY A SWORD

Sometimes we feel our doubt is a ferocious dragon blocking our further advance on the spiritual path.

At such times perhaps we are dealing with knowledge of God as if it were a legitimate problem of philosophy. Many philosophers seem to believe it is. But we make a fundamental mistake if we accept this opinion. Every philosophical system is erected by piling layer upon layer of reasoned argument, and knowledge obtained by such construction depends on discovering reasonable concepts about the existence and nature of God which must be further validated in testing.

Genuine knowledge of God as distinct from the philosophized is obtainable in only two ways: through the revelation of God in holy scriptures and the testimonies of saints, and through one's own immediate unitive experience of reality. The knowledge of God professed by most religious people is based on the act of accepting scriptural teachings as revelation. The knowledge transmitted by the saints of all religions is derived from their personal experiences of God-realization.

The knowledge from both revelation and direct experience is said to originate from a source beyond the province of normal reasoning; this knowledge can be acquired only intuitionally at the spiritual level, which is that of superconsciousness. And while this knowledge is sometimes presented and defended discursively in terms of reason, it is amenable to no such method, being irreducible to the level of logic. As the physical, emotional, and mental planes each have their own "language" of comprehension and expression, so the spiritual plane has its unique language, often a superconscious experience in itself, and this language has few or no translatable equivalents in any other. Spiritual realizations have to be understood and evaluated within their own field, rather than in the terminology of an incommensurate frame of reference. To illustrate the difficulty: try, for example, to convey precisely either in a painting or in a mathematical equation the hurt of a cut finger. How vastly more difficult is an intellectual explanation of the experience of "divine union" or *samadhi* [2] which, at the full, embraces all planes of consciousness and the totality of one's being.

We may doubt the wisdom of wholeheartedly and unquestioningly accepting the scriptural "revelation" of any particular religion. If we had been born in another part of the

[2] *Samadhi* (pronounced "sah-mah-dee")—Hindu term for the experienced realization of God or reality.

world, instead of drawing our main inspiration from the Bible, for example, we might be taking it from the *Koran*, the *Dhammapada*, or the *Bhagavad-Gita*. Yet we know that the followers of each religion tend to claim for their own scriptures *exclusive* monopolies of revelation. Can one ever know which "revelation" is the true one, or whether there is truth in all?

Now here, it seems to me, is why our doubt need not seem to be a dragon; and why, instead, we can use our doubt as a sword of discrimination.

First, we should not waste our energy attempting to do what the greatest philosophers have failed to do: to prove or to disprove the fact of God.

Second, as we undertake to tread the path of knowledge, we should accept its contention to test through experience that knowledge of God is truly available only in that consciousness which transcends reasoning. And we should expect to understand this knowledge only in its own language, which is not the hopelessly limited speech of everyday intercourse.

Third, if we are to seek whatever God-knowledge there may be, we will have to practice faithfully such disciplines as have the objective of leading us to the personal experience of divinity, at which point we will be better equipped to consider the degree of truth contained in "revealed" writings.

Fourth, we should constantly question (as distinct from criticize) every religious claim that seems counter to our own experience and common sense. And this entails the use of enough discrimination to know when to suspend judgment—when, for instance, to recognize that we may have a truth which is a mere fragment of a more inclusive truth.

Finally, if we are willing to test another honored hypothesis, we should remember we are told that those who ask, receive. We should make the experiment of praying: express our uncertainties as simply and wholly and honestly as we know how, and ask, of whatever God there may be, guidance into enlightenment.

Truly the eternal sword of the mind is the question mark. Honest doubt in an open mind is the first step toward gaining spiritual knowledge. Such doubt is never in conflict with the wise kind of faith. Doubt and faith, rightly used, counterbalance and correct the excesses of each other. For faith is the willingness to entertain a possibility, while doubt reminds us to accept only actualities.

6.   THE FAITH IN HONEST DOUBT

Tennyson's lines have a haunting, inspiring integrity:

> There lives more faith in honest doubt,
> Believe me, than in half the creeds.

Such doubt is the source of intelligent questions. Such questions point the way to a liberated spirit. So, in raising questions about the metaphysical distillations which may make one's denomination seem an essentially exclusive rather than inclusive organization, perhaps we should prepare to discover that our doubt may be leading us toward a richer faith. . . . I think of an old Negro whose church had recently been merged with a church of another creed—a fact that had led the old man to a line of larger speculation. One day when a census taker asked him, "What's your denomination?" he replied with thoughtful pride: "Ah'm no longer a denominator—Ah'm now a *straight* Christian!"

7. ON THE WANT OF PERSPECTIVE

There's a simple reason for standing back when we look at our beliefs. Get too close to a tadpole and you'll see a whale.

8. THE RELIGIOUS GROUP CLOSEST TO TRUTH

Which religious group seems to be closest to truth?

Let me first reply obliquely. If you want to know what is wrong with Protestantism, ask a Catholic; if you want to know what is wrong with Catholicism, ask a Protestant; and if you want to know what is wrong with Christianity, Judaism, Islam, Hinduism, Buddhism, and other religions, ask an exponent of each to give you his critique of the others. But if we want to know what truth is, I suspect we are going to have to dig it out for ourselves, and to find it revealed through our own experience. It is possible that, if we find it, we may discover the eternally changeless reality in all of these "wrong" religious bodies; and it is even possible we may conclude that somehow, in spite of theological differences, all sincere worshippers are heard by the same God. It seems to me that a healthy-souled approach to the spiritual life consists not of complacently adopting the nearest ready-made religious philosophy, but of following an intelligent method of discovering reality, of attaining unitive knowledge of the divine. As for one's allegiance to a religious group, I believe the best place to begin is usually where one is—and often that is also the best place to remain . . . with open eyes and open mind.

But now, to reply bluntly, the religious group that impresses me as being closest to truth is not any organized religious body but consists of those, from many groups, who have achieved the goal of all spiritual work: God-realization. And this group, I suspect one will inevitably discover, is less interested in the man-made differences of religions and more concerned with the transcendent unity of all in God.

9. THE TWO BRIDGES

I came to the void
that encircles heaven,
and found two bridges there.
And while I worried
over which to attempt,
a voice leapt the dark:
"One is for open minds
and one for open hearts.
Either will get you across!"

10. THE PATH OF LOVE-WISDOM

The greatest of all spiritual commandments is given in a single verb, and the noblest of all spiritual attainments is noted in a single noun, and both words are the same: *love!* Love God, love humanity, and love all creation. And your reward, when you have done this perfectly, is love itself; then, your nature is love, which is God's nature; then, in love, you are at one with God; and this, and this only, is God-realization. So that when you begin the spiritual life, and forever thereafter, the name of God which must be emblazoned on the heart is always this name, love. And love is all our excuse for seeking spiritual perfection, which is to say we seek the God-seed within us; and we seek self-realization in order to find God, and we seek God in order to find Him not only within ourselves but within all others and all the world. So that in this one word is all we must do, in it is all we must seek, in it is all we shall know, and in it is all we shall be—when, in Him, our name is His name: *love*.

Others believe the supreme spiritual commandment can be stated in this single word: *know!* Know thyself; know God; know thyself in thy God-nature; and in thy God-nature, know humanity and His creation. In perfect knowing you the knower, the act of knowing, and God the knowledge are one. So that at first the way of knowledge may seem to be in conflict with the way of love. Yet each is simply a point of departure, one emphasizing light and the other love; one stressing loving intelligence and the other intelligent love; one working through the head and the other through the heart. And both paths become one in the moment of spiritual realization, when perfect knowledge or wisdom is also perfect love, as if knowledge understood the sun and love experienced the sun's radiant warmth, so that the experience is really one of love-wisdom. Although the experience itself may be interpreted afterward in the terms used at either point of departure, the experience is of the same reality.

11. STEP BY STEP, FOR A MILE OR A THOUSAND

At times, when we measure what we know against what we do not know, and what we are against what we ought to be, we deeply despair. Yet, at just such times, we should remember how it was before we sought spiritual perfection at all.

Like the painter who, no matter how discouraged, keeps his vision of the masterpiece-to-be—like him, we have to perfect the parts to achieve the harmony of the whole. And at times, like him, we need most only to persevere.

"You cannot step forward with both feet at once," we are told; and "If you withhold the first step, the journey's never begun." Step by step, for a mile or a thousand, is how we have to go, however far the destination may be. Because more important than how far we have come is that we are on the way.

Like the snail who, the story goes, set out on a frozen January morning to climb the trunk of a bleak cherry tree. As he painfully fought his way upward a beetle poked his head out of a hole and advised him, "You're wasting your time, friend. There aren't any cherries up there." But the snail did not stop moving for a second. "There will be when I get there," he retorted.

3. THE STRANGER
ON THE PATH

I. THE ANIMAL-MAN AND THE GOD-MAN

Once there lived on a lovely and peaceful mountaintop a man who had been born a god-man. And there lived in the wild jungle at the base of the mountain a man who had been born an animal-man.

It was many years before either seemed to have any knowledge of the presence of the other. To the god-man, who was completely guileless and innocent of worldly ways, the first indication came when a great fire swept the jungle and extended part way up the mountain. For a moment or so he glimpsed a fierce-looking but terrified man-figure rac-

ing to escape the flames. And to the animal-man, cowering
in his cave one night when the beasts of prey seemed unusu-
ally active, the first suggestion of another presence came
when, in the moment of his deepest fear, he suddenly heard
—as if it were the momentary voice of the wind blowing
down from the mountaintop—a fragment of a song so noble
and so serene that his heart was mysteriously gladdened and
his fears somewhat subsided.

The god-man began to wonder how he might help the
animal-man, whom he knew only as a creature suffering
from a piteous terror. And the animal-man, whose lonely
and meaningless and fear-ridden life was a burden almost
beyond his capacity to endure, began to think with longing
of finding the source of the strangely inspiring song. It was
inevitable then, that since each had a deepening compulsion
to seek the other, they would soon meet.

And they did—one dawn when like a lane of light the
golds and blues and roses streamed down from the tranquil
sky. The god-man descended farther down the mountain
than he could remember ever having gone. And the animal-
man ascended farther up the mountain than he had ever
dreamed was possible. And the god-man paused on the edge
of a tiny sunlit clearing, his beautiful countenance shining
with love and expectation. And the animal-man stepped out
of the dark woods with his memory of the song still over-
shadowing his fiercely rooted fear and suspicion. For several
seconds, which seemed detached from time, they gazed at
each other, until the startled animal-man, overwhelmed with
an awe such as he had never known, felt his awe turning
swiftly into the more familiar fright of the unknown, and

then he bolted back down the mountainside as if attempting to outdistance the terror he carried within himself.

But now, when his fears returned, the animal-man would remember with quickening heart the vision he had seen of a godly being, of one who clearly had no fear of anything, who walked calmly and at will among the lurking dangers of the mountaintop, and who had looked upon him with such tender concern as the animal-man was incapable of comprehending. And so one day, when his courage had returned, the animal-man ventured back hopefully to the clearing. There, luminous in his dazzled eyes, was the god-man smiling and awaiting him. But again the animal-man, in a confusion of feelings, was unable to remain, although this encounter was a little longer than the first.

And each day the god-man waited patiently, and each day the animal-man grew more confident. From the shelter of the woods the animal-man began to tell the god-man of his fears, of all the terrors in the jungle which constantly threatened him. And the god-man listened, his compassion welling forth at these strange things whose existence he had never suspected. And because he discovered quickly that the animal-man was not yet capable of understanding much of his language, he tried to help by demonstrating his friendship, by striving subtly to transfer some of his strength to the other, by sometimes singing a line or two from one of his songs, or speaking a few simple words, or standing with hands raised in blessing when the animal-man came to stand before him momentarily, blinking as if blinded by a celestial light, then hastened away again.

This extraordinary relationship between the two persisted

for many, many years. But gradually they lengthened the duration of their meetings; the animal-man slowly overcame his timidity and awe; and the god-man found it increasingly easy to make the other understand him. At last a day came when they decided to become constant companions, and so they settled together in the little clearing, which began to ring happily with the irrepressible communication between them.

One morning after several years, while in the middle of a conversation where the silences had become more meaningful than speech, they stopped—struck by an incredible discovery. For a long time, in total wonderment, they stared at each other. Then, almost disbelievingly, the god-man whispered, "I now have all your knowledge of the jungle world." And the other murmured acknowledgment, "And I now have all your knowledge of the mountaintop world." And in that moment each saw how these two worlds were parts of a single world. And in that moment, as they stared at each other, each perceived that the other was his identical image; and, with that realization, they knew they now even shared the same mind! What I must do now—the purposeful thought flashed forth—is to live and to serve in both worlds. . . .

Then, while one strode with sure and happy step down the mountain into the jungle world, the other with equally joyous determination ascended towards the mountaintop world. And in the two worlds which were one world they too were one.

So it is of any man, of the meeting within himself of the higher self and the lower self. In full consciousness these two take from each other until they become fused in the totality of spiritual being.

2. DON'T EXPECT A ONE-DAY CROP

In the early stages of spiritual practice we tend to expect what is properly a later crop. We know that knowing God can come suddenly in a second, and we wonder why that time can't be now . . . like the village boy who planted a peachstone and sat down with his hands over his head to protect himself from the falling fruit. We, after a small nurturing of our spiritual seed, look up hopefully, perplexed that the saintly self doesn't immediately appear.

Yet there are many preliminary results which we may reasonably expect. For instance, to establish the habits of meditation, study, and service so firmly in our lives that nothing can tear them out. To control our desires by controlling our emotions and thoughts, to lead them instead of having them chase us. To develop a right attitude that makes us perennially calm and dauntless, regardless of whatever external events befall. To clarify and to ennoble our aspiration, and to reflect it in the least as well as the largest activities we undertake. To increase our self-knowledge and, by it, our degree of self-control. To make our life more creative, to place it within a larger plan of life. To begin with wisdom to give ourselves to others, and to taste the joys of selfless service. To begin to do God's will as we understand it, with intelligent love the expressive power of that will. And, in a mind that is becoming pure enough to invite Him, to sense His presence drawing near.

3. THREE TALES ON THE IMITATION OF THE HOLY

A starry-eyed young woman, who had accumulated a small religious vocabulary, rushed up to her spiritual teacher, and gushed ecstatically, "Isn't it simply fantastic! To think I have a divine soul slumbering within me!"

"Sh-h-h-h!" the weary teacher is said to have replied. "If you listen closely you can hear it snoring."

"Suppose, monks," a Buddhist guru addressed his followers, "an ass follows close behind a herd of cows, thinking: I'm a cow too! I'm a cow too! But he is not like cows in color, voice, or hoof. In just this way, monks, we have some monk who follows close behind the Order of Monks, thinking: I'm a monk too! I'm a monk too! But he lacks the desire to undergo the training to achieve the higher morality, the higher thought, and the higher insight which the other monks have. He just follows close behind, thinking: I'm a monk too! I'm a monk too!

"Therefore, monks, you must train yourselves thus: to have keen desire as you undertake the training in higher morality, higher thought, and higher insight. This, O monks, is how you must train yourselves." [1]

A robber was surprised one moonlight night (an old Hindu tale begins) while attempting to break into a village headman's house. But being a quick-witted fellow he

---

[1] Retold with minor variations from the ancient Buddhist text *Anguttara-Nikaya.*

noticed, as he ran outside, a large pile of ashes beside a distant pond. Swiftly stripping to his loincloth, he plunged into the water, burying his clothes in the mud, then sprang out and rolled over in the ashes.

By the time the headman had waked the other villagers and the search was on, the robber had run to the edge of the main road and seated himself in meditation posture under a holy *peepul* tree.

Late in the course of the hunt, as several villagers approached the tree, one suddenly cried out, "See—a holy man! Surely he can tell us where the robber is!" "No, no!" another villager hastily cautioned. "Can't you see he's in samadhi? It would be evil to disturb him. We must wait." Gradually, as the search cooled, still more villagers joined those who were waiting, until at last the whole village was assembled.

And now the robber, feeling he could no longer delay, dared the slightest peep. He was astonished to see how patiently, how reverently, the villagers waited for his counsel. More confidently, he sighed deeply in a manner that he desperately hoped would suggest his reluctance to return to the mundane world from more blissful regions. He slowly opened his eyes wide, and a shiver of anticipation thrilled through the crowd. For a full five minutes he gazed in apparent abstraction at a spot over and behind their heads. Then, lowering his gaze and seeming to notice them for the first time, he addressed the villagers in a low voice that was as gracious and solemn as he could make it: "Why do you search for a poor robber, my children? Better by far you should search for God!"

At these words of wisdom the villagers were overcome. They prostrated themselves at his feet. Then some ran off to bring back flowers, and others returned with leaf-plates heaped with such food delicacies as the village could provide. While the villagers begged him to remain, to bless their community with his presence, the robber thoughtfully distributed a little of the food to everyone, while eating heartily yet with a show of absent-mindedness. Then, thanking the villagers and smilingly declining their invitation to stay, the robber arose, impressively blessed them all, and walked quickly—but not too quickly—away.

Ah, the robber thought, this holy life is even better than being a thief! How the people respected me! Flowers and fine food—and given without my even asking, much less stealing! And how easy it is! Surely, as of this day, I change my profession!

For many weeks, highly enjoying his new life, he sauntered from village to village, always receiving ample quantities of food and esteem in exchange for his few harmless platitudes. But one morning, entering the largest village he had yet visited, he unexpectedly encountered a genuine young sadhu. The youth seemed delighted to see him. "Are you also on pilgrimage to Banaras, Saintly One? Then let us go on together!" After a few moments of thought he amiably agreed. This young fellow, he told himself, has a happy well-fed look, he ought to be able to teach me many useful tricks.

The journey might have been made in two weeks. Instead, it required closer to two months. The young man seemed to have a special ability for finding out every temple, however small or obscure, along their way and for leading his companion into them, where it was then necessary to spend hours in chants and songs and meditation. For six weeks the older man, in spite of his habitual distaste for sitting too long in one place, approved of the visits, feeling they lent authenticity to the role of holy man. But one day, as he and the sadhu left a temple with a group of lay worshippers, he was conscious of an ache in his back and suddenly rebelled, "I would avoid these temples for a while!"

And then, from a fleeting expression of puzzlement, the young man's face turned worshipful. Falling to his knees, he cried, "My guru—you are indeed my guru!" And rising swiftly, and turning to the group that had stopped to watch, he declared, "Instead of your beautiful temple, my guru now requires a cave. I beg you to help me serve him!"

After that experience—after seven days on a near-starvation diet while throngs of people huddled before him day and night to kindle their little flames of faith from his apparent bonfire of it—the former robber emerged from the cave another man. For, during that week, as he went through the motions of prayer, at some point he became conscious of the consequences of his deception, of the enormity of it, and he began to pray in earnest, begging forgiveness of God, first for his sins as an imposter, then for his crimes as a thief, and then for every wrong he had ever done that he was able to recall. Finally, to the youthful sadhu and the crowd of worshippers, he quietly confessed his story.

While some wept and all praised his newfound integrity he departed alone for the city. But he had traveled only a short way when the young man overtook him.

"Are you also on pilgrimage to Banaras?" he asked, his voice choking.

"Aye," the onetime robber replied. "To seek a guru."

"May you find him," the youth said happily, "as I, my guru, have found mine!"

Each of us can discover his true self, we are told, if he will develop the habit of holiness. One of the best ways to do this is to imitate those who have achieved the state of holiness. There are three kinds of imitation. One can imitate their words, their casual behavior, or their disciplines. If one imitates their words and casual behavior he will continue to deal only with his own inner emptiness. But if one imitates their disciplines he will eventually outgrow his imitative self and, even though he may have been a thief, begin to walk in the way of the saint.

4. THE ACTOR

In an ancient amphitheater
into which I lost my way one night,
I was astonished to see actors
by the thousands acting their way
through the roles of one man's life;
and the man, with face in his hands,
wept in despair at the very center.
"Friend," I asked, "which is truly you?"
"They are all of them me!" he cried.
"But I can't bear to be any of them . . ."
As he lifted his tear-stained face
I knew—I knew—it would be mine.

5.   THE REINCARNATED TIBETAN SAINT

Deep within oneself, how does it feel to be told that you
are a reincarnated Tibetan saint? I have met several such
saints, and all except one seem to accept the pronouncement
of their saintliness easily and without question. The exception was a lama who, in his early thirties, was the abbot of a
monastery in southeastern Tibet. This young *tulku*, "emana-
tion," whose title is *Rinpoche*,[2] "Preciousness," was notified
of his saintly nature while still a small child, and was taken
away at once by lamas to be trained in the monastic schools
of Lhasa. After graduating from the Lhasa schools, the
Rinpoche came to India for further studies. When I asked
him if he would mind telling me what he himself believed
about his saintly reincarnation, there was a touch of longing
in his look. "Wiser ones than I say it is so," he replied, "and
usually I believe it. But there are times," he added wistfully,
"when some of my meditations stray. And then it isn't the
saint whom I am said to be that I want to know, but who I
truly am, and who that little boy was, before the lamas came
to my parents' door."

6.   SUFFERING AS A HAPPY STATE

Finally you are becoming aware of the Stranger on the
Path, the spiritual giant within you, and to identify your
inmost self with him. And the restlessness that results from
these first contacts fills you with a frustrated craving to have

[2] Pronounced "reen-poh-shay'."

his full strength at once. It seems to you that if you could only make one inspired superhuman effort—one vast upward surge of strength—you would suddenly stand free, you would stand tall and calm and smiling, you would be the self you know now that you *can* be.

"If I could only be my best self," you say desperately. "If I could only break free—" Yet, you ask, how can you—how, today, can anyone? You dream of a springtime of the spirit, but you see a hard winter in the hearts of men. You dream of a time when men will trust in Man, but you see the doors and walls by which we shut each other out. You dream of a day when human values will be those of God, but you see the conflict between transient and timeless values dividing the world against itself. And feeling all of this struggle within yourself you despair—and yet, you sense the inner power that can set you free.

Once, to an old spiritual teacher, a pupil put the same question. And this was his heartening reply: "Won't you recognize that actually you are suffering a very happy state? Because now, by discovering your bonds, you begin to suspect what liberation may be."

How to see this—that actually you are suffering a very happy state? Why are you aware of your weaknesses? Because you are newly aware of your strength. Why does your mind remind you of your worst? Because your heart now whispers of your best. Why are you so distressed by the imperfections of the world? Because you have glimpsed a better world within yourself. Then, while you acknowledge the pain you feel, won't you try to perceive its happy cause?

The spiritual giant within you, of whom you are increasingly aware, needs time to liberate himself. He must not strain to burst all his bonds in a moment, but must untie them patiently, one by one, for many years. For many years, he remains on his knees.

Then one day, tall and calm and smiling, he suddenly stands free.

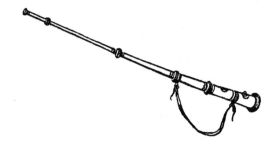

4. HOW SPIRITUAL
TRANSMUTATION WORKS

I. THE PEOPLE WHO ARE LIKE US IN THE
KALIMPONG BAZAAR

I wish you could have been with me in the Kalimpong bazaar. What, we might have asked each other, could we possibly have in common with the dozen varieties of exotic-looking people always found there?

Four tall Tibetans, with friendly-fierce expressions, have drawn apart at the far end of the bazaar. They crouch, stand, and squat about a small square of worn oilcloth, casting three dice. All are garbed in voluminous woolen gowns, one of crimson, one of blackish brown, two of dark blue, with sleeves which, when not pushed back as now, hang a foot beyond their fingertips and, in the Tibetan cold, serve the function of gloves. The crimson-robed one wears a high round heavy Tibetan hat, its crown richly embroidered against cream-colored felt with slender green-stemmed scarlet flowers, and with a great floppy bearskin brim of four petal-like pieces. All wear black soft-leather boots, bordered at the top with red felt. Their hair is plaited and coiled around the head, and the single braids of several of them end in dark red or amethyst-colored tassels. Each wears a large gold and turquoise earring in one ear, and a smaller turquoise ring in the other. As I watch, they are joined by a muleteer, just in from Tibet with a mule train probably bringing in raw wool. A swashbuckling fellow, with braided red-tasseled hair and earrings, but dressed in black trousers and a yellowish open-collared shirt. He greets the others with gusty good will and quickly enters the game. Somehow they remind me of a cheerful group of pirates.

A few doors away a Bhutanese youth is entering the little dispensary; and his business there seems to have to do with a dirty bandage tied around the calf of one leg. He has a strangely indrawn and surly self-sufficient look, an old-man look, odd in one so young. A short and stocky fellow, he wears a heavy homespun garment, of fine vertical stripes of browns, yellows, and white; he wears it like a bulky bathrobe, tied about the waist, but with the robe blousing down over the belt, because the skirt has been pulled up to hang just above his knees. His black hair is carelessly long and looks as if, when the mood strikes him, he must cut off a handful of it with his heavy knife. He makes me think of a young-old gnome, living in a gnarled ancient tree deep in a forest.

A sleek young Chinese woman passes, rustling in pale-blue silken pajamas; and her glossy hair, knotted in a bun, is decorated with an ivory comb. She smiles at the small girl with her who skips along, carrying a schoolbook. They pass by like fragrant flowers; and in contrast to the working clothes of most others in the dirty bazaar, they seem especially fresh and lovely. For a moment they glance in my direction, their black up-tilted eyes luminous with mirth, and then the little girl whispers something and they giggle happily and rush on. Chinese flower-fairies, I think, on their way to a fairy-school, surely, in a secret fairy-garden.

Two Bengali men idle through the bazaar; both wear white shirts of the high neckband type, with the shirttails flowing not far from their knees; and the older wears a loosely draped loincloth, and the younger wears white pajama pants. The older and larger of the men is declaiming rather pompously to the other, who listens with an almost fawningly respectful manner. Perhaps I imagine it, but both seem secretly attentive to their impact on others in the bazaar. The older man takes out a silver cigarette case; and after the merest suggestion of offering a cigarette to the younger man, who hastily declines, he pauses and makes a rather elaborate ritual of lighting the cigarette. The important man, I decide, holds a small political office, and perhaps his companion works for him or hopes to.

A Nepalese family, which has probably come many miles from a tiny mountainside farm, enters the bazaar quietly. The small-boned, wiry father walks several paces ahead; he wears a loose-hanging blue shirt, tight-fitting white cotton jodhpurs, and a beautifully brocaded black pillbox hat. His wife has a faded pink blouse, an equally faded green wrap-around skirt that hangs to her ankles, and an old yellow shawl wrapped around her waist and draped from the front over her left shoulder. She wears a silver anklet on each foot, silver bracelets on each wrist, a heavy necklace of silver coins, a dainty hoop of gold in each ear, and a gold ornament like a miniature marigold in the pierced side of a nostril; but her most unusual piece of jewelry is a silver ornament attached to the underside of her nose and bobbing down over her upper lip. A boy of about ten is clothed in khaki shorts and shirt; and a girl of perhaps eight is dressed much like her mother. The wife and children carry a heavily loaded wicker basket on the back, supported by a stout band which runs over the head, so that they appear to gaze in perpetual humility at their feet.

Small groups of lamas in dark red robes, some counting their 108 rosary beads and softly chanting *"Om Mani Padme Hum,"* [1] come and go between the bazaar and the Tibetan and Bhutanese gompas. Two fine-faced Hindu sadhus in flowing orange gowns approach the center of the bazaar, each carrying a small blackened beggar's pot. Farther away, surrounded by a curious crowd, is a "holy man" who has just walked here from Banaras; clad only in a skimpy loincloth and holding a six-foot trident, he has matted hair, long and unkempt, and his entire body is ash-smeared to a ghostly gray. And also in the bazaar as usual, and approaching several Indian visitors to announce his reluctant willingness to

---

[1] Sanskrit for "O the Jewel in the Lotus," variously interpreted—for example, as "O God in my Soul" or "O Absolute Reality in Man"; the most popular *mantra*, or prayerful invocation, used in the Himalayas. The *mantra* is often printed on prayer flags and also on paper which is inserted in Buddhist prayer wheels.

be photographed, is the simple-faced old man we think of as "the tourist's sadhu," dressed in many layers of clothes topped by a khaki-colored relic of a long coat, with a turban originally saffron but now almost white. He is bending under his load of framed pictures of various gods hanging from cords around his neck and from his waist, four or five rosaries draped over his chest, bells hanging from his waist, a lute tucked under one arm, a teapot and a beggar's bowl suspended from the other. Now he moves forward with a worried smile, one hand manipulating noise from a small tantric drum, the other tentatively extended palm up toward the tourists.

And there are others along the shop-fronted street of the main bazaar below us, along the side streets of the poorer sections of the bazaar, and in the large market area with its open-sided stalls and sheds down the hill. Groups of Bengalis, Tibetans, Nepalese, Sikkimese, Bhutanese, Assamese, Chinese, a few Europeans, and such regional groups as Lepchas, Gurungs, Tamangs, and others. Young and old, poor and prosperous, happy and unhappy; from cloud-high farms and pastures, from bleak stone-hut settlements up toward the snowfields, from the jungles of the lower valleys, and from villages and towns of the mountains and the plains; Hindus, Buddhists, Muslims, Christians, and people of the "tribal religions," such as those who worship the Supreme Spirit said to dwell atop snowy Kanchenjunga.[2] There are merchants and silversmiths, cobblers and tailors, and pro-

---

[2] Kanchenjunga is still called "the untrodden peak." Before the successful expedition in 1955 led by Dr. Charles Evans attempted the 28,146-foot ascent, promise was given to the Sherpas, one of the groups to whom the mountain is sacred, that no climber would set foot on the actual summit. The promise was honored.

fessional men and laborers, peddlers, and fruit and vegetable hucksters—some of them selling such articles as yak tails, silver shrine boxes, gold-brocaded cloth, paper-thin rice bowls, painted clay images of deities, and great curved knives in stone-studded leather cases. Others look and buy and laugh and argue and stroll and congregate, as the slow-drifting stream of people continues, constantly renewing itself.

What innate psychology can we possibly share with such people?

In each of us, operating on the instinctual and subconscious level, are five fundamental urges—innate and unlearned impulsions to certain general lines of action.

Like the Tibetans, preoccupied with their game of dice, every normal individual anywhere on earth has a need of other people. The infant and the child are dependent on others for life itself; and, as we mature, our need of others becomes increasingly subtle. Man, we say, is a social animal. Living and working with others, he can achieve what he could never achieve alone. Out of this *social urge* arise desires for such things as group approval, belongingness, and social status. Out of it stems the fear of loneliness. Its wrong expression takes such forms as aloofness and inhospitality, or such social irresponsibility as crime.

The Bhutanese youth, like us, has a strongly developed *instinct of self-preservation.* He has to protect himself from nature, from others, and sometimes from himself; and he also has a larger need to try to make his life meaningful. The self-preservation urge has two aspects: our need to sustain and protect our life and our need to live more fully. It expresses itself, for example, as the desire for good health, for physical and emotional security, and for self-fulfillment. Out of it comes the fear of death. It is demonstrated wrongly in such traits as miserliness and cowardice, hypochondria, or such behavior as stealing or injuring others.

With the school-bound young Chinese woman and child we share the *learning urge*, the instinct to inquire. From infancy we begin to learn how to govern ourselves, how to fulfill our desires and needs, how to adjust to society; and this urge, integral to general intelligence, is frequently combined with the other urges. It manifests itself in us as wonder and curiosity, as a desire for self-understanding and the understanding of others and the world around us. It is also the source of the fear of the unknown, especially when allied with an undiscriminating imagination. We see it incorrectly expressed in superstition, lying, prejudice, intellectual arrogance, mental tyranny.

Like the older Bengali each of us considers himself a very important person, the true center of the universe; we share with him this *urge for self-assertion*. Man is an acutely self-conscious entity, filled with esteem for individuality. Each of us cherishes his uniqueness and, at best, we become creatively expressive and begin to discover, beyond our personality differences, our spiritual identity with others. The self-assertion urge leads to the desire for recognition, the desire to be liked, the desire to be taken seriously. From it comes the fear of failure. Wrongly expressed it may appear as self-deception, vanity, the craving for power, as a sense of inferiority or superiority.

With the Nepalese we share the *unitive (or sexual) urge*.

We have a need to unite and identify ourselves with others, and with groups (especially the family) or causes (such as nationalism and organized religion) which seem to be greater than ourselves alone. This urge embraces all the differences which arise from the interplay of male and female psychologies. It leads us to desire companionship with those of the opposite sex, and, in most cases, to share our mature years and our love with a mate. And it also leads us to establish ourselves as a unit in a meaningful group (or groups), or to serve a significant cause, or to cast our lot with a strong and personally appealing leader. It gives rise to the fear of separateness —perhaps the most tenuous and the least understood of all fears. When wrongly expressed we recognize it as exhibitionism, the desire to dominate or to be dominated, sensuality, devotion to unworthy groups, causes, and leaders.

But now, you may ask, from where does the spiritual impulse come? Our spiritual motivation may be active at three levels: at the instinctual level, as the five basic urges impel us to follow certain lines of action toward positive development; at the conscious or intellectual level, as conscience and self-conscious spiritual effort; and at the intuitional (the superconscious or spiritual) level, as soul exerts its impact on everyday consciousness. Man cannot be spiritual in one aspect of his being and nonspiritual in the remainder. At the lower levels of being, however, the spiritual aspect is potential rather than realized; and the potential is released and fulfilled through self-purification and renunciation.

The five urges therefore represent spiritual potential; and this potential is realized by their right control and right use, and their alignment with our motivation at the conscious level and, finally, at the superconscious level. The five basic urges have to be transmuted deliberately, through the conscious mind, and harmonized with their spiritual or superconscious counterparts. Like the lamas, the sadhus, and the holy men, we have an inner drive in the direction of God. But, until we gain control of our instinctive energies, the spiritual drive will be all but lost in the noisy confusion of our self-centered interests.

Our innate urges operate largely as desires. And these desires are commonly expressed through our emotions, which means that the original urge may be more or less modified by our conscious mental faculties. At once we find our social background at least a temporary block to understanding.

Why, we wonder, should such virile specimens as the Tibetans wear earrings and dress their hair in tasseled braids? Why should the Nepalese father let his wife and children carry heavy burdens while he walks ahead carrying none? Somewhere in the developing course of the Tibetan and Nepalese societies, certain of the basic urges have been channelled into socially dictated expressions. We ponder, for instance, whether the Tibetan practice is based on the unitive urge and is the Nepalese custom a male expression of the self-assertion instinct? Are the Tibetan males striving to make themselves more sexually appealing to their females, and is the Nepalese father (like the old Bengali) attempting to indicate to others how important he is?

In a normal member of any society, the basic urges will be partially transmuted at the conscious level, and in ways generally acceptable to the society. An American girl might consider the Nepalese woman's nose ornaments odd and even amusing; but the Nepalese woman would find the American girl's battery of cosmetics (not to mention her hats and slacks) just as strange. And the American girl might also wonder at how a person of such a relatively low economic and social status could possess such ornaments. The Nepalese woman, who has never been permitted to own land or anything except personal articles, and to whom her jewelry is both bank account and insurance, would be perplexed perhaps as to how her less-ornamented American sister provided for the future.

Our understanding of others deepens, of course, as we learn to look beneath what they do to why they do it; and every why of human behavior has its ultimate root in one of the innate urges or a combination of them, or in its conscious or superconscious transmutation.

The expression of our urges may be very complex. Several or all urges may be given a combined expression. In composing a poem, a poet may be hoping to win the approval of others and to gain popularity (the social urge); he may be attempting to earn money so that he can eat more regularly (the self-preservation urge); he may be experimenting with a new verse form (the learning urge); he may be trying to prove his creative superiority to other poets (the self-assertion urge); or he may be addressing his poem to a young lady whose favors he longs to win (the unitive urge).

Social customs and practices, as we have seen, may direct the urges into devious and often obscure avenues of expression. Moreover, the urges become transformed with increasing subtlety as one advances in inner growth, until action sometimes appears contrary to the nature of the urges, and one is tempted to question whether the saint is any longer bound by the instincts. What can one say, for example, about the self-preservation instinct when a man willingly dies for the sake of others?

Here, then, is how we may begin to transmute our innate urges.

The key to control of the social urge, which impels us to establish physical, emotional, and mental relationships with others, is *right attitude*. Without right attitude our chance of getting along happily with others, and with ourselves, is slight indeed.

In transmuting the self-preservation instinct, which forces us to seek self-protection and to achieve a more positive state of life, we need to develop wise aspiration, or *right aim*.

As we begin to govern the learning urge, we work for *right knowledge*—especially self-knowledge, knowing that if we understand ourselves we shall be able to understand others.

The self-assertion urge, with its impulsion to express the unique self, is purified through *right creativity*, to express the spiritual self.

And the unitive urge, redirected toward union of the lower self with the higher self, and the soul-infused self with God, is fulfilled at the superconscious level, and the external sign of this unitive knowledge is *right action*.

These means of transmutation, in turn, form a chain. Right attitude must be directed through right aim. To carry out right aim we must have right knowledge. To increase our knowledge beyond the limited scope of reason we must develop right creativity, the capacity to utilize the intuitive wisdom of the highest levels of consciousness. And as we develop creative intuition we can begin to approach self-realization, or union with God, which expresses itself in right action.

Our instinctual energies do not simply wander away and vanish somewhere in the lower nature, like a stream disappearing in a desert. Man is a totality of being, and in the saint it is the totality which is purified and unified. In the spiritualized individual, the five urges are aligned harmoniously with the energies and qualities of the spiritual self; and the extent we can achieve this will be the degree of control we have over our total resources.

The social urge, deliberately transmuted through the will to enjoy, becomes the experience of joy and, at the upper reaches of consciousness, the peace and the bliss so constantly recorded by the saints. And the fear of loneliness expires when, through the awakening of spiritual group-consciousness, we experience the fact of our inner oneness with others. So with the other urges. How can the saint, who knows his real nature to be immortal and who is fulfilled in God, any longer fear death? How can the fear of the unknown bother one who knows the identity of self-knowledge and God-knowledge? How can the fear of failure concern one whose self-assertion urge has been transformed into the resolute determination to express God's will through the divine self? And how can the fear of separateness dismay one who is at one with God and who, filled with the love of God, spontaneously expresses this love in sacrificial service?

Consciousness is the innate capacity for relationships. We know that in the Divine Life (Absolute Reality, Tao, Brahman) all relationships are contained and resolved. Intelligent love then, controlling the urges and their conscious and superconscious counterparts, is our best means of expanding consciousness; because the greater love is, the more inclusive it becomes. Through it we begin to identify ourselves with others and the world; until, as we progress through the stages of higher realization, we begin to know the increasing perfection of all relationships in the One Life; until, in this growing knowledge of how the One Life pervades all that which is, we find ourselves in God and express God-nature in our being and in our doing.

The innate psychological makeup of human beings everywhere is the same. The same instinctual energies, fears, and needs move all of us; and the same spiritual resources are potential within us. The same psychological processes in all of us must be understood, controlled, and developed; because, whatever our religion or race, self-purification is the essential condition required of those who seek to know God or reality. The practices which lead to self-purification are similar in all religions because the same ideal preparatory state of being is sought by all. And so, if we will look closely enough at the people in the Kalimpong bazaar, we will find something of ourselves in them, something of them in us: at one level, our common humanity and at another, our common God-nature.

2.   THE FIVE GREAT YOGAS

Once, in an ashram in Madras, I heard a beloved saffron-robed old swami explain the five great yoga systems of India in this way.

"According to the *Upanishad*," he began, " 'As the birds fly in the air, as the fish swim in the sea, leaving no trace behind, even so is the pathway to God traversed by the seekers of Spirit.'

"Yet," he explained with a smile, "if the birds and the fish know where they are going, then as they depart there is some first trace of their pathway. So with yoga, the discipline which we hope will 'yoke' us to God. Each yoga is a trace of the beginning of the pathway.

"There are five main approaches to God. Now, imagine we have five yogis, each following a separate path. Suppose a maharajah invites each in turn to visit his treasure room and to help himself to two handfuls of the treasure. How will each react?

"The *hatha* yogi follows the way of physical perfection. He wants to still his body so that the Self may be heard. He enters the treasure room. At once, instead of seizing precious gems, he spies two nearly empty heavy iron pots which will be useful to him in his exercises. With great effort he lifts these and leaves.

"The *bhakti* yogi follows the way of intense devotion. He tries to make himself a perfect servant of God. Once in the room, he takes great pains to select the jewelry which will make the most beautiful decorations for his favorite image of God. And he also manages to take a little money with which he will buy flowers, incense, and oil lamps for use while making his devotions.

"The *karma* yogi follows the way of selfless work. He attempts to perform his everyday duties perfectly, giving all the fruits of his labors to God. He studies the treasures in a businesslike manner. He carefully selects only the smallest items of the greatest value. He will use his new wealth to assure the security of his family and to support his guru and favorite temple.

"The *raja* yogi follows the way of constant, dedicated meditation, as taught by Patanjali. He wishes only to be perpetually conscious of God. He has no interest in visiting the treasure room. Once there, he scarcely seems to see the fabulous collection of valuables. He turns away to go back to his meditation place. He seems not even to notice that, as he steps from the room, someone has pressed a few coins in his hands.

"The *jnana* yogi follows the way of wisdom. He aspires to understand how it can be that everything which exists is contained in the One Life. He is delighted with the treasure room. He sees every article, from the smallest to the largest, as a reflection of the beauty and the mystery of the Life of God. He thinks, as he views the various items, how he himself is contained, even as the treasures are, in the all-embracing Life of God. He departs empty-handed, the treasure room held in his mind and heart.

"These are the five approaches," the old swami said. Then, his eyes sparkling, he concluded: "But once a person has gone far enough along any of these paths he discovers the other ways begin to fuse with his own, so that, in the end, all ways join, and no trace is left as the self disappears into Spirit."

3.   SINGLENESS OF PURPOSE

The minimum basis for seeking self-fulfillment is to believe in your capacity for growth and to take the action necessary to release your potentialities.

From seed to blossom the plant grows with singleness of purpose. So it must be with each of us, as we bring in the incredible power of the spiritual self, with the result that our lives may consummate in the full flowering of God-realization and of wise service to mankind.

4.   KNOW YOUR POTENTIALITIES

Abide steadily in the knowledge of your potentialities, derived from the scriptures and the saints and from your own experience. Be not easily dissuaded, as some are, by the shock of disbelief a new truth often imparts.

Two little caterpillars were having a very private discussion of the story passed on to them by a tadpole that some day they would become beautiful butterflies.

"Do you really, really think it's true?" one asked anxiously.

"At first I did," the other replied sadly. "Then that little fish had to spoil it by claiming that some day he's going to be a bullfrog!"

5. THE HEART OF SADHANA

I. THE HEAVEN AND HELL OF ATTITUDE

One day as an elderly swami and a friend of mine were walking through the outskirts of an Indian village, they came upon three children with tear-streaked faces in the act of burying what had obviously been their much-loved pet dog. The children had already dug a small grave, and the eldest was standing uncertainly while his little sisters collected bouquets of wildflowers. At sight of the swami and his companion the children tried to greet them, but their grief was too much and fresh tears flowed. Solemnly the old swami walked over to the graveside, taking the girls' flowers and arranging them carefully, and the children gathered beside him expectantly. It was a beautiful ceremony of touching farewell to a true friend who was now about to enjoy the extraordinary delights of a heaven full of woods and streams and things to chase and many titbits to eat from a never-empty bowl. At the end, as the swami departed, the children were so overcome with the little dog's good fortune that they were dry-eyed and chattering happily. When they had walked down the street a way, my friend commented on how swiftly, thanks to the swami's tenderness, the children's attitude had swung from one extreme to another. "But they are just like us, you see," the old swami replied softly. "Happiness and unhappiness will always be in them, and will always want a little separating . . ."

But how much more complex is the matter of right attitude in adult life! With every triumph we soar towards heaven and with every failure we plunge towards hell. It is not life that can break us, but the constant extremities of our response to it. "I myself am heaven and hell" is a statement of basic spiritual truth. "As a man thinketh in his heart, so is he." We largely express—and determine—the quality of our life by our attitudes. These attitudes, compounded from such elements as desire, fear, feeling, emotion, prejudice, ambition, are fundamental in shaping everyone into the kind of person he is.

Nothing is pleasant or unpleasant in itself. Our outlook makes it seem so. A task is simply a task, its pleasantness or unpleasantness existing in our mind. The same is true with everyone and everything we consider. Pleasant and unpleasant people, for example, simply don't exist! People and things unknown to us occur as they are in themselves; and we change them, we create our own images of others, by our attitudes. Between ourselves and the world we place a screen of attitudes, and everyone and everything we regard is transformed in our own mind into a false picture, heavily distorted and colored by our own approval or disapproval, happiness or unhappiness, pain or pleasure.

Further, since we are normally attracted to those beliefs which reinforce our attitudes, our attitudes are more important than our beliefs. The basically pessimistic or optimistic individual, for instance, seems by a special magnetism to attract those moods and opinions which strengthen his attitude, while rejecting all others. We think of "poisoning the well" as a form of improper argument; as, for example, to call our opponent a liar and then to dismiss everything he says subsequently as a lie because he is a liar. But we constantly poison the well of life by our predetermined attitudes, which usually are deep-rooted in emotion and argument-proof against reason. Most of us, most of the time, respond like the little boy who was told his sister was naughty because she had plastered another child in the face with a mudpie. "She isn't naughty—" the boy replied indignantly, "she's my *sister!*" She can't be wrong—she's my friend. He can't be right—he's my enemy. It *has* to be right—isn't it *my* idea, *my* political party, *my* community, *my* religion—even, *my* God? Unless one is willing to labor for right attitude, one never gets even within the shadow of the true razor-edged path.

Falsity dies as right attitude is born. But right attitude obtains on many levels, each reflecting our interior growth. We begin to purify and to transmute the social urge, so that we can regard others and the world at large with an attitude which is outgoing, positive, open-minded, calmly and happily spontaneous, unself-conscious and, at its best, self-forgetful and selfless. We build right attitude by steadily evoking and sustaining the quiet type of true enthusiasm, the will to enjoy, which eventually blends with detached intelligent love. Then one is above both happiness and unhappiness, pain and pleasure, and sees with unobstructed objectivity into the soul of all things.

By consistently evoking the will to enjoy, we achieve the attitude necessary for undertaking spiritual practices; and this attitude, as we fuse it with intelligent love, enables us to progress through dispassion to discrimination and then to detachment. It teaches us to be sensitive to the seesaw balance in us between such extremes as happiness and unhappiness and pain and pleasure—to be aware of how, so often, these extremes are only in want of a little separating. It teaches us that our choice to live in heaven or hell is a matter of attitude, that we can go through life unloving to hell, loving to heaven. And it makes real for us the truth beautifully expressed in the ancient Tibetan *Tanjur:*

> Whatever happiness is in the world, it has arisen from a wish for the welfare of others.
> Whatever misery is in the world, it has arisen from a wish for our own welfare.

2. TRUE ASPIRATION INVOLVES PERSPIRATION

When a faultfinder asked the Buddha why he failed to give the secret of salvation to everyone, the Buddha suggested the man go from door to door to find out what people wanted most out of life. On the man's return the Buddha asked what he had discovered.

"Their wishes," the man said, "are for power, fame, wealth, beauty, popularity, happiness, love, good health, long life, and such things."

"Did any wish the secret of salvation?" the Buddha inquired.

"No one," the man replied sorrowfully. "No one at all."

"Then how," the Buddha asked, "shall I force on them what none wants?"

Fortunately some people, perhaps few enough to be missed even today on a quick door-to-door poll, do want the secret of salvation, or of self-realization.

Yet, the religious interest of many of us seems often to run in proportion to the size of our troubles. I think (fondly, I confess) of the steward on our mine sweeper in the South Pacific during World War II who once, during a tense moment, suddenly relaxed us all by blurting out fervently— "When Ah gets home to Lou'siana, Lawd, Ah promises You Ah'se goin' to church every Sunday for a week!" And I remember another time when, as our ship was returning to port after being badly battered by a storm, the toughest man aboard, a burly Irish boatswain's mate, came up sheepishly to ask permission to go to church. "I figure," he explained wryly, "I'd better stab at getting a little holier—for the duration, you know."

What in life do we want so much we will give up all else to have it? Aims such as those the Buddha's critic discovered? Or a greater goal?

When I think of aspiration I like to remember the inspiring bronze statue by Philip S. Sears at Fruitlands, outside of Harvard, Massachusetts. Many times, high up a hillside overlooking a great green sweep of valley, I have sat to meditate on this statue of a soul-in-his-face Indian, He-who-shoots-the stars, whose bow is drawn and whose dream-tipped arrow is at the instant of winging straight up into heaven. How often have I envied that brave his fixity of aspiration!

As spiritual aspirants we set a two-in-one goal: *the subjective*—to achieve self-realization, through love to know God and to do His will, and to work for this through self-purification and the release of such qualities of being as spiritual will and intelligent love; and *the objective*—to harmonize our outer life with the inner, and to find the type of service activity which best allows us to express our growing spiritual powers. The objective goal should provide a congenial setting for the quest of the subjective goal, hence the importance to aspirants of "right means of livelihood," one point of the Buddha's "Noble Eightfold Path." The work we do, spiritual teachers say, should be a means to an end and not an end in itself, and any aspiration short of God-realization is inadequate and limits our performance.

The emperor Akbar, who delighted in the singing of his court musician Tansen, asked the musician one day if there could possibly be a greater singer in the world. For answer, Tansen requested the emperor to accompany him to a simple hut beside a river. When they arrived Tansen introduced his old teacher, an ascetic, and asked him to sing. The old man did so. At the beauty of his singing Akbar was overwhelmed and conceded his superiority to Tansen. On the way back to the palace, a puzzled Akbar asked how such an old man, living in extreme austerity, was able to sing more exquisitely than a court musician, living in unexcelled luxury. "Sir, I sing for you, an earthly emperor," Tansen replied humbly, "but my master sings for the Lord of the Universe, and that is why his singing is superior to mine."

To establish right aim is not easy. It takes intensive introspection to determine our highest aspiration, to develop and refine it, and to keep it as pointed and living as the growing tip of a tree. True aspiration involves perspiration, but its discovery yields a rare new dimension of joyous living. "Self-realization," the *Katha Upanishad* declares, "can come only if from inside one's heart there spring purity of resolve and earnestness of spirit. It does not come by much study or by learned discussions. It comes to one whose better self yearns for realization, and whose mind has turned away from evil and has learned to subdue itself and to be at peace with the world. . . . Those of steady mind do not spend their thoughts on transient pleasures. They seek the joy of liberation."

3. SELF-KNOWLEDGE IS GOD-KNOWLEDGE

I sought Thee according to many counsels—
in stone and blossom, in moth and star,
in a seaside haven, in a mountain hut,
in church and temple, in ancient texts,
in men called wise, in living and dead,
and thy signs were radiant everywhere!—

while Thou, my Lord, for whom I searched,
for whom the futile pilgrimage was made,
awaited me in the still cave of my heart.

Surely this is where we seek Him best, where He is most
easily met and known. Acquiring self-knowledge is like being heavily blindfolded, then blundering around from place
to place, till one day, when at last the blindfold is removed,
we see we have only moved around unseeing in a place of
eternal light. God does not suddenly come to us, He has
always been there, in His secret place in our heart.

The inmost nature of everyone is God-nature. Self-
knowledge leads ultimately through meditation, study, and
service to the experience of this fact. We grow toward the
experience through three types of knowledge: instinctual
and subconscious; intellectual and conscious; and intuitional
and superconscious. Underlying our quest of the unitive
knowledge of absolute reality is the learning urge at the instinctual level, and at the conscious level the will to know.

What is the essence of the quest? The constant lifelong
meditation of Sri Ramana Maharshi (one of the greatest recent teacher-saints of India) revolved around a single question: *who am I?* Once, when an ambitious follower asked the
Maharshi if seeking political power for the sake of the country were a worthy goal, Sri Ramana replied: "Your duty is
not to be a patriot. It is *to be*." You are more than this changing body, he declared, and more than its fickle emotions and
transient thoughts. Something so incredibly indefinable in its
love as to be illimitable, inexhaustible, infinite. Self-knowledge can mean finally only the knowledge of God-nature.

The One inhabits all, Sri Ramana testified, and so you will know who you are when you know *You are That.*

Then no matter how beautiful the aspect of nature, how solitary the refuge, how hallowed the center of worship, how wise and inspired the scripture, how loving and enlightened the teacher, there is one place to seek Him which will always be easiest and best—in the unchanging part of yourself —in the "still cave" of your heart, where He even now awaits you.

4. HOW TO BE MOST CREATIVE WHEN LEAST CREATIVE

What do we actually mean by such statements as "Life is the greatest art" and "We need to live more creatively"?

One of my Indian friends, who is a poet, says, "I will be most creative when I succeed in being least creative." If you say, "But that's a contradiction in terms," he will ask, "But are you interested in expressing your personal will or God's will?" And if you confess you aspire to do God's will, he will reply, "This is my meaning, that the greatest creative artists and thinkers are those who most purely express His will. If one can negate himself sufficiently this becomes possible. Ah, then, where now is our esteemed self-expression or our originality or our creativity? Where except lost in the doing of God's will?"

He makes a challenging point, I think. In the scriptures of world religions, right creativity is, though implicit, one of the least discussed of all spiritual attributes. This may occur, it seems to me, because man has always tended to equate creativity with originality, and originality with individuality.

The scriptures insist on self-renunciation; and if one obeys, individuality and therefore originality seem to be thrown on the scrap heap with whatever is personal and material.

The most successful exponents of contemplation and also of action, spiritual teachers believe, are those who experience and express for others some aspect of reality, of that divine orderly whole pervaded by its own principles and laws. The experience of reality is an inexpressible fact—an experience totally surpassing any intellectual or artistic description we can give it. From the highest viewpoint, creativity begins when we attempt to express the significance of some facet of the Absolute. The reality to be described is One; our expressions of it are legion. As Emerson reflects: "Raphael paints wisdom, Handel sings it, Phidias carves it, Shakespeare writes it, Wren builds it, Columbus sails it, Luther preaches it, Washington arms it, Watt mechanizes it." And, I think Emerson would permit us to add, the saint *lives* it.

Theoretically, if you could express God's will perfectly, in all its love and wisdom and power, you as an individual would be completely noncreative, a channel only. In their moments of highest inspiration, great creative artists and thinkers, like the true saints, have cried out, It is not my will, but thine which has been done through me! All of them— from Philo and Fra Giovanni to Kabir and Jacob Boehme —have had their version of Blake's disclaimer, "The words are not mine!" Practically, however, when we labor to express the infinite and eternal we must do so through form, whether of art, science, behavior, or whatever; and form immediately imposes finite limitations. And that reality which cannot be limited is, through the illusion created (as in a poem or work of philosophy), expressed in a form and in a style which at best may suggest the nature of the boundless, somewhat in the sense of attempting to explain the ocean to a blind and deaf person by having him stick a finger in a glass of water.

To be true to one's true self, one has to transmute the self-assertion urge, through the conscious will to create, into a superconscious or spiritual expression of one's God-nature. One begins by wanting to express himself; when successful, he ends by expressing God.

The greatest creative artist or thinker works in the image of the Creator, in this way: Divinity, as nearly as man has been able to comprehend, expresses itself first in will which produces purpose; then in love which provides method, procedure, an energized relationship between original purpose and the purpose manifested; and finally in active intelligence, which works out the purpose and method in creative activity. For example, the will to good is expressed through good will and becomes the act of good will. All creative activity follows this three-stage process: purpose, method, manifestation.

Purpose is discovered at the spiritual level through intuitive perception of God's will. St. Francis heard a voice directing him, "Repair My church." The purpose requires the choice of right method. His general method, St. Francis knew, had to be that of love; specifically, he determined to procure the necessary materials and to work on a little church near Assisi which had fallen into disrepair.

Then, purpose and method have to be fulfilled by the work of active intelligence, to master details and to make the inner purpose outwardly tangible. St. Francis begged the building materials necessary and, with his own hands, succeeded in restoring the little church to its original beauty. Later he was to discover that the "church" mentioned by the voice applied to the entire Christian Church then established.

We can see this three-stage process demonstrated in every phase of human activity. For instance, someone will have the aim of founding a school; then funds and buildings and equipment and staff are provided as the method of expediting the purpose; and finally purpose and method are fulfilled as teachers address their classes. And in a corporation, for example, a policy (purpose) is formulated, procedures (method) are determined, and thus certain practices are established.

Life is the greatest art in the sense that a saintly life is the best expression of eternal truths; and to live more creatively means to express our divine nature more effectively. If one perfectly expressed God's purpose, used His method, and achieved the created thing willed by Him, then my Indian poet friend would be correct. From the viewpoint of the lower self, one would be noncreative; but from the viewpoint of the spiritual self, one would be most creative: in one's identity with God, one would be sharing the work of the Creator.

5. LOVE IS MY GOLDEN TOUCH

"Go out of your house in the evening," a wise man told a loveless youth, "and give your heart to a rose and a bird and a stone."

The youth never returned. Instead, after many years, a young man arrived whose face was a lover's, and whose simple robe was a monk's.

"And what did you find?" the wise man asked.

"I offered my heart as suggested," the young man replied, "but at first I could not get it accepted, except by a lonely child. And then a lost dog took it. And then an old beggar woman, after a while. Until I began to notice it was easy, if you gave it to those who had no love or who had not love enough. So one day, beginning to see how it was needed, I decided I might just as well give it to all I met. And suddenly while offering it freely, even to roses and birds and stones, there came from heaven a chorus of voices, led by the sweet voice of a child. 'The heart you offered to us,' they sang, 'has been accepted by God.' "

In this is the secret of self-realization: love experienced, then love expressed. Through meditation, study, and service we seek the unitive love-wisdom of God. We try to transmute the unitive urge so wholly that we can be at-one with God through our God-nature. The sign of this experience, which is the sure mark of the saint, is that after the experience its love-wisdom quality must inexorably be expressed. The experience, which leaves its shining imprint on one's entire being, is channelized through the will to good, the will to serve. Selfless service is simply love-wisdom, or intelligent love, in action; and this is the essential meaning of right action.

Once, while talking with one of those sweet-voiced, sweet-tempered Baul singers, I asked, "How do you believe liberation is achieved?" "Only by death," he replied seriously.

Then, gently smiling, "By *death-in-life*—by dying to all except Him. How are we able to do this? Listen . . ." And he sang:

> "Love is my golden touch—
> it turns desire into service:
> Earth seeks to become Heaven,
> man to become God."

And this is why right action is based on love. Because love pushes you out of yourself, making room for God. Love pushes you out of yourself, making room for others. So that through love—your "golden touch"—you never try to put your soul into the world, but to take the world into your soul.

6.   SADHANA

What is *sadhana?*

Imagine yourself at sea on a fiercely stormy night, struggling in a tiny craft to reach an almost unattainable rock islet washed over by waves, but surmounted by a dark lighthouse; at last, somehow, reaching it, you ascend through total dark the shaky unfamiliar rungs of a ladder, slipping, clinging, climbing. And then reaching out in the blackness, you suddenly, unbelievably, fumblingly touch and turn on, flood and shatter the fearful night with a blinding white blossom of light . . . If your journey is the journey of the spirit, and your achievement of self-realization the instant the great beacon is lit, then all your efforts, all your discipline, all you have done to reach the light, this is sadhana.

Sadhana comprises all the practices we follow to attain

the experience of the God within. The literal meaning of the Sanskrit word is "that by which something is performed," the means to attainment, the method. Sadhana may be thought of as the immediately practical aspect of the spiritual way; as the disciplines—in particular, meditation, study, and service—by which we tread the way; as the techniques by which we transform hypotheses into the living truth of individual experience. Sadhana means, in brief, a fully disciplined life in quest of the experience of God-realization.

The heart of sadhana is the development of the five aspects of inspiration—rightness of attitude, of aim, of knowledge, of creativity, and of action—through right use of will and intelligent love. These five aspects are cultivated, beginning at one's present stage of consciousness, through the disciplines of meditation, study, and service. This is how we realize the spiritual power-potential within us, and become finally what God intended us to be. When that day comes, instinct, intellect, and intuition function as one. Then we act as one with Him.

6. OPEN MIND, OPEN HEART

I. A TALE OF FIVE LAMAS

A wise old lama, who had agreed to become the abbot of a newly opened lamasery, saw that all the monks were novices and would require extensive instruction. He desired to have several teachers and especially an assistant abbot, one who some day could succeed him. So, to a friendly brother of his order who was the abbot of another monastery, he dispatched a message requesting that five candidates be sent him by a certain date.

His friend duly selected five promising young lamas and sent them forth. And the five lamas, elated at the prospect of freedom after years of unbroken monastic routine, set out on the three-day journey over rough mountain trails, reveling in the blue and white majesty of the mountains, the curve and roar of snow-fed streams, the high rocky pastures and the tree-shaded valleys, and particularly the chance to see and speak with many new people.

Late the first afternoon, several hours after having stopped for a happy chat with a group of villagers, they were ascending a steep flowering valley when they came abreast of a pretty little house set far back from the trail, and beside a grassy banked stream. As they paused, with the melodic rushing of the water making them aware of their thirst, the youngest lama thought he heard a voice hailing them, so they walked toward the stream. And thus it was they rounded the house and came out on the bank of the stream and, to their own astonishment, startled a girl, more beautiful and certainly more lightly clad than any angel they might ever have dreamed of, in the midst of her bathing. As the lamas averted their gaze, she sprang from the stream and hastily pulled a long garment over her glistening body.

While the lamas fervently murmured their apologies, the girl, her poise now somewhat regained, insisted they enter the house for tea. And though the afternoon was waning, and they knew they should return to the trail, they agreed to tarry to please the girl.

But as they sipped their tea, conscious of the girl's efforts to be gay, it seemed the girl was really attempting to conceal a feeling of distress. And after a while, seeking the cause, the youngest lama asked, "Your parents—are they away for long?"

In an instant the girl's forced gaiety was gone, leaving traces of fright and despair. "I may as well tell you," she blurted out, "I want you to spend the night—my parents are away—there are bandits and I—I'm terribly afraid!"

But the lamas explained they must be on their way, and they urged her to seek safety elsewhere.

She looked at them unhappily. "My parents made me promise to stay and take care of the house," she said. "But why cannot one, just one of you stay?" she pleaded, as if she were about to weep. The grief in her eyes, as she fleetingly sought the youngest lama's help, entered into his. "I promise," she whispered, sobbing, "if—if you stay, you'll be—very glad—"

At once the older lamas protested, saying she was justified in sleeping at a neighbor's house and that this was what she should do. But the girl refused, covering her face with her hands, and giving herself up to convulsive sobbing.

"Go ahead," the youngest lama told the others. "I will stay. And perhaps if I hurry I can overtake you tomorrow."

The older lamas argued with him. But he would not hear. And his glance returned again and again to the weeping girl. At last, unable to dissuade him, they arose and went sorrowfully on their way; and their distress was increased by the girl's last words to the youngest lama coming faintly to their ears, "You won't care, will you, if I go and finish my bath—" As they climbed towards the far head of the valley, one of the lamas made a suggestion; and then silently they prayed for the girl and her protector.

The next afternoon, while walking outside the wall of a prince's great mountainside stronghold, they were accosted near the gate by a richly dressed retinue. A proud-faced young man, garbed in a gown of scarlet silk, invited them in a commanding tone to enter the gate and enjoy the prince's hospitality. But the lamas demurred, explaining their need to hasten on.

"Then hear why you are welcomed," the young man declared haughtily. "The prince immediately requires a religious ceremony to be performed, but the family lama has been called away. The prince has authorized me to enlist a lama's services at any cost. Look!" he said persuasively, opening a leather pouch and slowly pouring silver coins into a large palm. "I will give you these now and, afterwards, some gold."

"We must not be tempted," one of the lamas said softly to the others. "Come quickly, let us go."

The young man sensed the lamas were about to leave. "I will give the one who stays twice as much!" he cried. "What a royal gift to take your abbot! And think of this, if you please the prince you may be invited to join the household. I assure you, you would find this a most lenient place, with such riches and foods and drinks—such public and private amusements—as you can't even imagine could exist."

One of the lamas, turning to the others, said excitedly, "We must stay! Think of how our gift would please the abbot!"

"I give you your choice," the prince's representative declared. "You can be foolish and go hungry on your way, or you can be wise and be rewarded if you remain."

"I will stay," the excited lama told the young man. "But only overnight—or at most a few days."

In vain the others tried to change his mind. But the eager lama was already joining the retinue, and the imperious young man caught the lama's arm, and then the group went shouting and laughing through the gate. Sadly the lamas resumed their journey, adding a new name to their prayers.

During the morning of their final day of travel the three lamas entered a small town. And having eaten nothing since noon of the previous day, they took their bowls and went to beg for food from door to door. Collecting enough to make a meal, they sat beneath a tree to eat. They were just finishing when a large coarse-looking fellow, with several boisterous companions, swaggered up.

"See the parasites!" he shouted. "See the lazy beggars! They don't work and yet they eat! Where's the justice of it?" he cried angrily, as a crowd began to gather. "What fools we are! We break our backs—for what? To feed an army of deadbeats!"

The lamas arose; and one, asking for silence, smiled humbly and said, "In many ways you may be right. It is by your grace we eat, though none is forced to help us. I promise you we shall take what you say to our hearts and search it for helpful truth. Now, if you will forgive us, we must continue our journey. We are expected at a certain place this evening, and the distance is still great."

Respectfully the crowd parted for them and they began to walk away. But their accuser was not finished.

"Look at the cowards!" he called contemptuously. "They're afraid to talk! See how they crawl away—like puking dogs!"

Anger flushed the face of one of the lamas. "I won't leave!" he whispered fiercely. "I'll reason, I'll fast, I'll pray, and I'll show him he's wrong!"

They tried to persuade him that the man's remarks were not directed against him personally, that it was futile to reason with such a person, but that later they might return and speak more calmly with their accuser. Their efforts were useless. Finally the two remaining lamas strode up the road, adding a new prayer.

It was shortly after nightfall when they plodded wearily into the lamasery grounds. A youthful monk, who had been posted to meet them, ushered them into the abbot's quarters.

The old abbot came forward, his smile warm with love for them; and after giving them his blessings, he inquired about the other lamas. They tried to explain, pleading for understanding, "It has been so long since we have had such freedom, reverend sir. Our brothers are devout men who intended only well—certainly no wrong." The abbot said nothing, but his understanding and pity were apparent.

"We have prayed for them," one of the lamas said. "My brother here thought of that, his faith being that it would help."

The abbot nodded, studying the two lamas. Then, to the last speaker, he said graciously, "Now tell me what you want and you shall have it."

"A little food and much sleep," the lama replied promptly, with a tired laugh.

The abbot called to a monk outside the door, giving him instructions. The hungry lama left at once.

Turning to his companion who still remained, the abbot inquired kindly, "And what, my son, is your wish?"

And the young lama, the most quiet and pensive of the five, who had urged his companions not to fall behind, and who had defended them before the abbot, now looked into his superior's questioning eyes and spoke what was in his heart.

"I am here, my reverend abbot," he said slowly, "only because my being here was promised. I beseech you, please do not make me stay! Let me rejoin my brothers who with a little help will be more quickly free. My holy father, that help is a small thing—let me go!"

The old abbot suddenly seated himself, peaceful and smiling. He spoke quietly. "Five of you started. Four had dispassion; three had discrimination; two had detachment. But only one, my son, only you had compassion. Yes, you may return, but in the morning. You will find them in good hands. Because, I confess, this was my way of testing you." He smiled tranquilly at the astonished young lama. "Sit down with me and rest awhile, my son—my successor."

2. FIND HIM WHERE YOU ARE

One trait of the saint is his development of totality of being. He is neither introverted nor extraverted, yet he is both; neither contemplative nor active, but both; neither an idealist nor a pragmatist, but both; neither an intellectual nor a lover, but both. He looks at comedy and looks at tragedy, and sees these as the changing faces of relative truth; he sees the world, himself, and others as transient manifestations of the Absolute. He neither goes into himself nor out to others; for him the inner and the outer realms have become one. He neither forces himself on others nor withdraws from others; he sees himself in the world and the world in himself. He erects no barriers between himself and others; his heart and mind are open to all and to everything; his love is a bridge between opposing men, and his life a bridge between man and God.

It is this equilibrium and this harmonious state of being that every aspirant seeks. But he has to seek it in the place where his duties and obligations lie. That place may be a mansion, a single room, or a hut; in a city, on a farm, or in a forest hermitage; among crowds of people, among a few, or alone. By doing his duties without attachment to result or reward, by doing his duties cheerfully and freely and fully, however noble or ignoble they may seem, he learns to dedicate himself to God. His duties, he soon realizes, are to the God-self within himself and others, and to the Supreme Life which is the Life inspiring every form. As he balances his time between meditative and study periods alone and engaging in business and social affairs with others, between pursuits of the mind and the cultivation of the heart, between aspiring and doing, and between doing and being, he gradually develops facility for using any part of his total resources which circumstances may require, until at last he is prepared to do whatever God may require.

3. HOW TO OPEN THE SOUL TO GOD

One of the richest rewards of living in India has been the opportunity to know some men who unmistakably know God. One of these, a guru of seventy who looks little more than forty, summarized for me the key to his spiritual effort: "An open mind and an open heart open the soul to God."

There is no other way, when one thinks about it. An open mind gives and takes truth, an open heart shares love. And without truth and love we can never know God.

These pairs—mind and heart, truth and love—work together more intimately than we are apt to realize. "As a man thinketh in his heart" is the technique we need; not "As a man thinketh in his head." And similarly it is not just "love" we need, but intelligent love.

Yet, how we close both mind and heart with our strange prejudices!

Take skin color, for instance. How do you suppose we became the way we are? According to the Nagas, a hill tribe not too distant from Darjeeling, God made a model of man and slipped him into the oven; but being new at the job, He took him out too soon—and the pale and pasty creature became the white man. The next time, fearful of making the same mistake, God left him in too long—and the burned-looking fellow became the black man. But the third time, knowing exactly what to do, God took him out at just the proper moment—and the beautiful golden man who emerged was, of course, the Indian.

Many people would contend, I imagine, that cherry trees blossom in spring, marigolds in summer, chrysanthemums in autumn, and poinsettias in winter. But in the eastern Himalayas that is not so. They bloom simultaneously in November. And not only that—while some trees are shedding their leaves, and others getting them, grapefruit and bananas are ripening in the garden.

Unhappily most of us seem unaware of how many of our notions are preconceived, both big and little ones. When asked how he had formulated the theory of relativity, Einstein replied: "By challenging an axiom." We need to challenge a great host of opinions we regard as axioms, instead of seeking false mental security in inflexible attitudes. Opinion is born when thinking dies. Emerson mentions a famous teacher who used to plead with his students: "Don't ask me what I thought a year ago on this or that; ask me what I think today."

Instead, we ought to be prepared to accept truth wherever it turns up and to take it to heart. C. T. Studd, one of the first missionaries to reach the central region of Africa, illustrates this in telling how he converted a cannibal chief through the chief's wife. One day while talking to the chief and his wife, he dwelt at length on how God is a God of Love. When he had finished, wondering if he had made an impression, the wife turned to her husband and declared emphatically, "I always said there ought to be a God like that!" Studd, too, responded to truth wherever he found it; in fact, his interest in Africa was first aroused back in a London mission office, where he was intrigued by a note pinned to a bulletin board: "Cannibals want missionaries."

To be open in mind and heart means to be objective, and to be objective is to act and react while remaining detached as an observer. This is why spiritual preceptors in every religion stress the necessity of controlling desire, emotion, and mind. We are permitted to evaluate but not to condemn, it is said. I have often wondered how radically different our behavior might be if we knew that some time after death we would have to sit in a celestial theater, and there, in the company of the heavenly hosts and all our acquaintances, witness a motion picture of our entire life! Should we not be detached enough to begin now to produce the life story we would prefer?

Invariably a trait of those who have openness of mind and heart is a keen sense of proportion. This probably accounts as much as anything for their sense of humor. St. Teresa's humor remained with her even when she was on the verge of losing her life. As an elderly woman, while crossing a flood-swollen stream, she fell in the water and was swept away, floundering in the raging channel. "Is this the way You treat me?" she asked God. She heard a voice reply, "But sometimes this is how I treat My friends." St. Teresa managed to gasp, "Then no wonder You have so few of them!"

Once we get this openness of mind and heart, we also achieve a new and unshakeable poise. A friend once told me about a psychiatrist who had such poise. One day a mentally ill man rushed into the doctor's inner office, brandishing a pistol, and shouting, "I'm going to kill you!" The psychiatrist looked up momentarily from some papers and demanded sternly, "Do you have an appointment?" The man confessed he didn't. "Then," the psychiatrist said stonily, "see my secretary and make one. Nobody sees me without an appointment!" The man departed meekly to comply.

Not long ago I heard that a Kalimpong friend, a lovely old lady who lives alone on a widow's pittance, had paid a very high price for an embroidered table cloth which I was sure she did not need. After some persuasion, she explained the piece was made to order by a penniless widow with several small children. I remarked on the subtlety of her selflessness. "It has always seemed to me," she said gravely, "that love is best when its reasons are hidden from sight. Besides, see how happy I am," she added, her eyes twinkling. "Is it not true that love delights the giver more than the receiver?"

I have heard many good things from the wise men of India, but none wiser than this: "An open mind and an open heart open the soul to God."

4. THE BHAGAVATA AND THE BROTHEL

Two friends were out one evening looking for something to do, according to a favorite tale of Indian sadhus, when they came to a crowd listening to an elder read from the *Bhagavata*. "Why don't we stay to hear?" one man urged. "Perhaps it would profit us." But after listening a few minutes, his friend became restless and left. He finally ended up in a brothel. Soon, however, he became disgusted with himself. "How worthless I am! Next time I'll stay to hear the word of God, like my friend, instead of doing a thing like this." But the friend who was listening to the *Bhagavata* also became disgusted. "How foolish I am! Next time, instead of listening to some dull fellow read, I'll go to a brothel and have real excitement." It happened that a storm came up and the two friends, rushing homeward, met on the way; but the storm grew more violent and they hurried to take shelter beneath a large tree. Scarcely had they reached it when the tree was struck by lightning and both men were killed instantly. The Messenger of Death came for the soul of the one who had listened to the *Bhagavata* and dragged him off to hell. And the Messenger of God came for the one who had visited the brothel and led him into heaven.

Truly the Lord looks into a man's heart, Sri Ramakrishna comments on this story, and judges no one only by what he does or where he goes.

5.   THE PRISONER

Raving through the streets
ran the prisoner, clutching
bystanders who struck him away,
beseeching to be told, weeping
to know if he were free.

Raving out of the city
ran the prisoner, chased by
the dogs of sullen laughter,
pleading with the air
to cry out he was free.

"Stop, mad friend," whispered
a voice that was nowhere
the raving man could see.
But the raving man shouted,
"Sane one, come—tell me!"

"All are enslaved—" the voice
sighed, "cast out from where
all should be. Storm the soul!
And when you seize what is there,
go back—set the prisoners free."

7. WHAT IS MEDITATION?

I. AN INTRODUCTION TO MEDITATION

Man's most ancient, most universal, and most successful means of attaining salvation, of fulfilling his spiritual potential, of perfecting himself in God, of experiencing reality, is right meditation.

This is the testimony of the saints of every religion. It is the conclusion evident in thousands of years of spiritual history. And this is the great truth proved daily in the transformed lives of men and women everywhere. Except I find Thee in my meditative heart, the saint cries through the ages, I search Thee in the world in vain!

Meditation is the open secret of those spiritual leaders and exemplars who have radically altered the moral and religious character of humanity. Meditation, they have taught, is the foundation of all effort for liberating the greatness latent in the soul of each of us. The Kingdom of God is within; God-power awaits in every man; loving meditation is the one path straight to Him.

Why then, when such a method exists, do relatively so few religious people use it?

The answer seems to be that many people equate meditation with prayer. Some even appear to regard it as an idling away of odd moments in a kind of pleasant "spiritual brooding." The fact is, however, that prayer is only one aspect of meditation; and far from being a type of rarefied daydreaming, meditation is an intensive and even difficult discipline which at first may require a tremendous output of effort, an effort at the highest point of consciousness we can sustain.

When we pray, one who meditates will say, we ask God to solve our crises; when we meditate we learn to solve them for ourselves. When we pray we speak at the conscious level, sometimes emotionally, sometimes reasonably; when we meditate we attempt to reach a further plane of consciousness, the intuitional or superconscious level. When we pray we talk to God; when we meditate we aspire to become one with God.

In the prayer of petition (a plea for ourselves), intercession (a plea for others), or adoration (an expression of devotion to the divine), we look outside ourselves, to God Transcendent. As one of its stages, meditation may include any or all of these classes of prayer; but true meditation always involves inlooking to God Immanent.

One of the simplest forms of meditation is to repeat a prayer slowly and reflectively, then to take a word, a phrase, or a sentence and to concentrate on extracting its spiritual meaning, especially seeking an intuitive insight into the experience of its truth. For example, when meditating on compassion, we strive not for intellectual understanding alone, but for the experience of being compassionate.

Other simple (but not easy) forms of meditation include the prayerful repetition of a name of God, in which one seeks to identify himself through his divine nature with God; the repetition of invocations such as "Enter my heart, O Spirit of Love"; and the attempt to answer such questions as "Who am I?" In all of these, as in concentrating on an extract from a prayer, we endeavor to gain an intuitive or experienced knowledge of the truth being meditated.

There is nothing hit-or-miss about the disciplined practice of meditation. You meditate daily, usually early in the morning and again in the evening, and normally for about fifteen to thirty minutes each time. You follow a carefully planned program of meditations, designed to meet your immediate needs, and to effect the safest and speediest development of wholeness of being. You observe a definite physical procedure. Sit comfortably with the spine erect, head neither raised nor lowered, eyes closed to minimize distractions; and do this in a place which affords solitude and silence. And in spite of your conviction that you have been thinking all your life, you must learn how to think, to concentrate, before attempting to lift your awareness to loftier levels of consciousness. A profitable suggestion for the beginner is to try to concentrate for twenty to thirty minutes on a single subject, such as spiritual aspiration, without permitting the attention to waver.

Is it possible, the question is frequently asked, to learn to meditate effectively without receiving personal guidance? The answer depends on how dedicated, intelligent, and hardworking one is, and on what written instructions are being followed. It *is* possible—and many people who meditate are largely self-taught. However, one can obviously derive inestimable benefit from working with an experienced counselor, and this is the better way. Certain systems of meditation exist in every religion which can be undertaken only with expert instruction. And there are also forms of meditation, intended for those doing advanced work, which are transmitted orally only from teacher to pupil. If these meditations are used too soon or wrongly they are far more dangerous than helpful.

Most systems of meditation employ a graded sequence of meditation forms. When a meditation form is mastered— this may take a few months to many years—one graduates to the next and, at least temporarily, more demanding form. The first forms used are intended to produce a calm, stable, well-integrated personality, to fuse the physical, emotional, and mental components of being into a spiritually purified and disciplined whole. Later meditations are planned to awaken intuition and to lead to the state of consciousness often called the soul-infused self; and others represent a direct all-out effort to achieve the unitive love-wisdom experience of the Absolute. In conjunction with these general meditation forms which deal with the whole self, more specialized forms are sometimes used for other purposes—for instance, to develop dispassion, to eliminate fear and anxiety, or to perfect various capacities, such as creativity.

Finally—to reply to another question commonly raised—must you be a religious person in order to undertake meditation? "If you had asked me about meditation," St. Teresa says, "I could have instructed you and advised anyone to practice it even though he does not possess the virtues, for this is the first step towards obtaining them all; it is vital for all Christians to begin this practice." Meditation is not for perfected people, but for those who seek perfection in God. Any normal person, whatever his outlook on the spiritual life, can prove for himself in a short time how beneficial to his happiness and well-being meditation can be. For those whose aspiration is high, meditation will provide the most direct and the most practical method of achieving self-realization. It will help one to make himself capable of doing God's will, and then to discover what His will through one actually is.

In consecrated meditation the life in God truly begins. Except I find Thee in my meditative heart, each of us, sooner or later, has to learn to say, I search Thee in the world in vain!

2. SANCTUARY

Why have aspirants of every religion, in every age, sought out monasteries and convents, and retreats hidden in deserts, jungles, and mountains? When a man might make a comfortable mansion his goal, why does he choose instead the severe simplicity of a lonely cell, a tiny hut, or a cave?

Spiritual silence is possible at first only in a sanctuary. In the physical environment itself, there must be the conditions of solitude and silence. "Let the ascetic be alone," an old Buddhist text admonishes. "It is enough that he has to fight with himself."

But what is this silence which is so precious to the lover of God? Once, on his way to a secluded clearing near the top of our mountain, I met a sadhu who clutched a rolled up deerskin (his meditation mat) under one arm and a small cloth-wrapped bundle, probably of food, under the other. The man's intense suffering was visible in his frail slumping body. Later I met him again, descending the trail—but was it the same man? This man came down the trail with the easy grace of an animal, and his whole being radiated a kind of luminous tranquillity. What had he found in his silence?

The struggle to proceed from external quiet to internal calm consists, according to many teachers, of four types of silence. There is the silence of environment, the silence of mouth, the silence of desire, emotion, and mind, and the silence of God. These are progressive stages in achieving complete detachment from the world and the self so that, at the final stage, only God is present in meditation.

But many aspirants protest that living continuously in solitude and silence is, for them, out of the question; and even obtaining such privacy and quiet for an hour daily is in fact almost hopeless. Many have to live and work in noisy cities and towns; many share an apartment or room with others; many are married with small children in the home. What can you do if you have a problem such as one of these?

First, whatever our environment when we turn to the spiritual life, it is in that place we must begin. Whatever our duties are, it is these duties we must perform better than ever. Not many aspirants are able to have ideal conditions of work at the start, and few spiritual workers ever attain them. It is even debatable whether long periods of continuous solitude and silence would be desirable for most aspirants. But the minimum necessity—fifteen to thirty minutes for morning meditation and the same time for evening meditation—really must be fought for. How can solitude and silence be found for these two brief periods?

Here are solutions which some of my friends have devised. One meditates daily, on his way to work, on a park bench; one meditates in a church which is always open; one, who shared a three-room apartment, moved to a single room; one arises an hour earlier than the other members of his household; a city couple designates an area of their bedroom, partly enclosed by furniture, as "the meditation corner"; a couple with children moved from a city to the quietest section of a suburban district; a couple added a special small room to their home to be used only for meditation and prayer; and one couple, living in a desirable but noisy section of a large city, soundproofed a small room they use for meditation.

Your meditation place, whatever its size and location, ought to be a carefully guarded retreat reserved for communion with God. In it you never fret over petty matters; it should be held inviolate for the pursuit of spiritual affairs. It should not be a place of light conversation and argument, any more than should a church or temple; the shrine should induce in you, the moment you enter, a sense of deepest reverence, serenity, love. You do not invite friends to it indiscriminately; it should be opened only to those who will enter into your spirit. It should not be a show place for religious art objects; it should be as simple in appearance as your chastest taste permits. Unnecessary noise, even unnecessary conversation, is not allowed; a silence perpetual and peaceful enough to invite the Voice of God is the unspoken rule.

Then, when you have created such a place, and when you have consecrated it through wise use, you will discover one day that this sanctuary has enabled you to find another. You will find in the deepening silence, as the sadhu who visited our mountain found in his, a sanctuary from which you will never again be separated, which will always be open to you, whatever crowds and noise surround you. And this new sanctuary will be the inmost calm center of being, the refuge in the heart and the garden of the Beloved, in which your communion with Him is unbroken, to the eternal refreshment of your soul.

3.   THE NEED FOR SOLITUDE

The right meditation place can make a vast difference. Once, when I was spending a week alone in a high Himalayan valley, my meditation on a ledge near a cave (which I was considering moving into) was interrupted one morning by a pleasant-faced young forester, carrying a shotgun. "Please forgive me, sir," he said apologetically, "but I thought you might be interested to know that only a few mornings ago, near that cave behind you, one of my men spotted a full-grown bear." I told him I was somewhat interested and did not mind moving at all.

4. AS FOR SILENCE

The abbot of a gompa on the outskirts of a small village, a Buddhist friend tells me, was surprised one day to see a lama, known for his faithfulness to meditation practice, borrowing the much-used new drum of a neighborhood boy. "But I had no idea that you could play the drum," the abbot remarked to the lama later. "I can't," the lama replied gravely. "But now —neither can the boy."

5. THE FIVE LEVELS OF MEDITATION

There are five great steps to the unitive experience of God-realization. Often, but not always, these stages are consecutively achieved.

Concentration is the use of the conscious mind, holding awareness steadily to a subject. It includes both concrete and abstract thinking. The all-important foundational phase of meditation is learning to concentrate. Unless the conscious mind is controlled and can be made to do your bidding, the quest of higher stages of spiritual consciousness is futile.

Reflection is the use of the conscious mind with some use of the subconscious mind. More rarely, awareness may be centered in the subconscious independent of contact with the conscious. Much that is claimed to be spiritual originates during reflection when the subconscious, given a task, throws to the mental surface its best spiritual content—forgotten and often undigested material about the spiritual life. Much that is creative, sometimes spectacularly so, also occurs during reflection or in its potent aftermath, when insight is gained into previously unperceived relationships.

Contemplation is the use of the conscious mind with some use of the superconscious mind. Contact with the conscious mind may cease and awareness be focussed in the superconscious only. This is the stage where true spiritual realization is first experienced; when connection is made, at first, as a rule, momentarily, with the spiritual self.

Intuition is the use of the whole mind—the conscious, the subconscious, and the superconscious. There is an enormously enhanced freedom of consciousness because of the great scope of intelligent relationships discoverable among the three areas of the mind. Intuition, in a sense, is a more sophisticated version of contemplation, because it tempers the heavenly material of the superconscious with the earthy stuff of the subconscious and conscious. Normally an intuitive insight bears this mark by its acceptability to reason and common sense; and the ultimate test of every intuitive realization, sooner or later, is its practicableness and reasonableness.

Illumination is the perfected use of the whole mind in rapport with the universal mind, or mind of God, and reality itself. This is the crowning experience of the meditative life, the self-realization which is God-realization. However, there are various degrees of knowing, even on this one level. The experience may be of the personal God or of absolute reality. In the first stages there is awareness of one's relationship to God; in the higher stages there is no relationship, no perception of duality, no knower or lover, no knowing or loving, and no God to be known or loved, but only the indescribable Supreme Life Self-Aware.[1]

From this I believe you can begin to deduce the probable level of origin and the significance of many of the phenomena sometimes encountered early in the intensive practice of meditation.

One may hear voices or music; one may see visions, geometric designs, colors, lights, fiery symbols; one may smell rare fragrances; one may converse with "spiritual entities" visible or invisible; one may be flooded with joy, peace, love, "divine intent"; one may be lightning-struck by a truth of utter clarity and simplicity. One may also have, much more uncommonly, a negative experience—of obstacle and opposition, of deep-rooted fears dramatized and even personified, of an oppressive undercurrent reaching for the self, and of an insidious sense of one's own spiritual importance.

As you will guess, most of these experiences occur at the level of reflection. The subconscious assists the conscious mind, both areas usually containing an intense craving for vivid spiritual experience, to glamorize, sensationalize, and generally distort ordinary material into an experience imagined to be laden with spiritual significance. The experience seems especially convincing if one slips out of the conscious world and into the subconscious dreamworld during medi-

[1] Various individuals and schools of meditation give other descriptions of the stages of meditation. But the stages described here may, I believe, be more readily understandable and acceptable than some of the more traditional (and even antiquated) descriptions.

tation. In this realm of make-believe, where the original
spiritual motivation preserves much of its strength, one experiences wish-fulfilling dreams or, though infrequently,
even nightmares. With relatively few exceptions, experiences with sensory phenomena fall into this category, as
does much experience which is popularly accepted as being
genuinely mystical. Normally with a valid intuitional or
superconscious experience the sensory overtones are added
after the experience, as the conscious mind desperately attempts to retain, to understand, the remembered and almost
indescribable experience. Most of the sensory phenomena
met with early in meditation practice—voices, visions, fragrances, "spiritual entities," and the like—are wishful products of the subconscious mind.

True spiritual realization at the level of contemplation is
apt to come first as one of four types of experience. It may
come as an inrush of sublime love, peace, bliss, spiritual
purpose, which later almost inevitably refocuses the personality at a wiser and more loving level of consciousness. It
may come as an intuitive insight, as a sudden revelation of
some aspect of truth which has either eluded or been beyond the grasp of reason; but this type of experience often
brings special dangers to the individual not prepared for
them.[2] It may come as a sense of a Spiritual Presence—the
inmost self, of God-nature, of God. Or it may come, although this is not an infallible sign of a contemplative experience, as light—diffuse light, a blaze of light that rises
and falls, a sun the size of a pinpoint, or a pinpoint sun with

[2] The section which follows deals with this problem.

a dark center. Occasionally, and for comparatively few people, one of these early experiences may be marked by a loss of bodily consciousness—but not of awareness itself, which becomes exceedingly acute. The aftermath, even after many similar experiences, is marked by a sense of painfully deep shock as consciousness returns to the unreality of the everyday world.

6. BALANCING THE DISCIPLINES

Is it true, as one often hears, that formal meditations are not really necessary, provided you maintain a meditative attitude throughout the day?

The suggestion is actually a very ancient one, stemming from the lazy schools of every religion. One short-lived Chinese Buddhist school carried it even further. It attempted to eliminate not only the superconscious activity possible through meditation, but all possible mental activity as well. (Perhaps the quick expiration of the school ought to be regarded as a testimony to the success of its members.) While the practice may indicate deep self-deception, it usually seems to be a temporary rationalization of one's lack of earnest spiritual application.

Every meditation should be a period of intensely concentrated and undistracted self-development and God-search. In one of the higher stages of meditation (contemplation) one enters areas of the superconscious where all awareness of the external world may be lost; yet these experiences afterwards starkly illuminate the external world. In still

more advanced meditative experiences, one goes through
the subjective world, to a stage of love-wisdom, where the
objective world is re-entered; but now all illusory distinc-
tions fade away, and inner and outer, the interior and the
exterior worlds, are experienced as one, arbitrarily divided
by the analytical mind.

It is this new ground won in meditation that we strive to
make the common ground of everyday consciousness. The
narrow strip of the conscious mind is widened, and we
achieve this by reclaiming for the conscious mind the
ground of consciousness which formerly belonged to the
subconscious and superconscious realms. To be fully enlightened is, in this sense, to widen the conscious mind until
it includes the vital content and capacities of the subconscious and superconscious, until the whole mind is always
available for use. As this state of being is approached we
simultaneously, in complete awareness, destroy more and
more of the unreal barriers between what we call the internal and the external worlds.

It is true that the general all-day attitude sustained outside of meditation by the spiritual adept has a meditative
quality. And it is also true that his norm of consciousness,
even in the midst of worldly activity, is at a far higher
spiritual level than that of aspirants during their meditations. But the spiritually great have testified that their everyday level of consciousness has reached its advanced point as
a consequence of meditation, with its gains necessarily sta-
bilized and balanced by study and service. The great saints
and spiritual leaders have never believed nor taught that a
stage is reached when one might wisely abandon the system-

atic practice of meditation. How then can a novice of the spiritual life dare to dispense with it?

Why is it not enough if we only meditate, or only study, or only serve?

Meditation, study, and service, as they contribute to our wholeness of life in God, are as inseparable and as essential to each other as the three phases of breathing. Meditation, like the breath inhaled, is a time of intake; study, like the pause between breaths, a time of balanced quiet; and service, like the breath exhaled, a time of output. "What a man takes in by contemplation," Eckhart declares, "that he pours out in love." And hear Ruysbroeck: "God aspires us into Himself in contemplation, and then we must be wholly His; but afterwards the Spirit of God expires us without, for the practice of love and good works." Between the replenishment of meditation and the exhaustion of service is the restful calm of study which looks to both meditation and service and is their unitive force.

More specifically, in meditation we evoke energies which have to be given creative expression. Study and service teach us to understand these energies and to use them constructively. However, it is quite possible to arouse this energy before the lower self is fully prepared to handle it. Many people, not just creative artists but workers in various fields, including science and religion, have learned how to evoke but not how to control this energy, and the results have sometimes been disastrous. The problem is that, to a mind unprepared by self-purification and loving intelligence, superconscious insight may have a deeply disturbing effect; and if the experience is often repeated, the cumulative impact of these truths taken by violence may be more than the nervous system can bear.

There are many other reasons why these three disciplines must be balanced if we are to achieve a healthily developed fullness of being. In meditation we explore new areas of consciousness; through study and service we make them habitable to our normal state of consciousness. In meditation we ascend to new heights of love and wisdom; through study and service we learn to give right expression to our rich and sustaining realizations.

In study we vicariously share the experiences of those who have entered realms into which we are still advancing; we learn how they have made practical applications of the truths illumining their lives; and we are then better equipped to progress in our own meditation and service. We carefully analyze ourselves, weighing the emphasis given to meditation and service, the balance between introversion and extraversion, energy evoked and energy expended, and reason and love.

In service, which expresses the quality of our being, we utilize all we have gained in meditation and study. We know because we serve, and we serve because we know. In service we live every moment in the nourishing knowledge of our oneness with others in God, knowing that love given to others is love given to Him.

We should be faithful to our spiritual disciplines—and remember them particularly when we are troubled. Why? They give us our moments of greatest sanity and of maximum detachment and intelligent love. There is no spiritual growth without them. Even on the rare occasions when we cannot afford the full time necessary, even then—especially then—we should hold the mind to a formal meditation as long as we can.

And we should hang onto our sense of perspective. This means, whatever we do, we should never let go of our common sense and sense of humor. As a Sufi saying puts it: "When the heart weeps for what it has lost, the spirit laughs for what it has found." So we should try always to identify ourselves with our laughing side.

7. DAWN MEDITATION

Every day at dawn I had gone down the valley from the village, past paddy fields and farmhouses, crossing the stream to where the forest of evergreens massed at the base of the mountain, almost concealing the thread of a path that pointed to the summit.

And every day, from the first dawn, I had become increasingly conscious of a certain symbolism in the ascent from the valley to the mountaintop, as if I had been led to this place by a desire to find the forms in nature which expressed an emerging reality of my inner life.

In the beginning I had lingered there in the valley, tempted to spend the day examining every appealing object —the sand of the stream like a silt of glass and gold, cat's-paw clumps of moss, black and rose and white pebbles, ferns like ribbed lace, tiny pale flowers like bells and stars, and a crumbling ledge with the profile of an old Indian's face.

I was late in climbing, those first few mornings, because

I was learning a new way of knowing these things; and sight and sound, fragrance, touch, and taste were exhausting themselves.

Each day it was easier to leave the vicinity of the stream. As I followed the path through a tangle of undergrowth, then into a dark cool tunnel that led upward beneath the evergreens to more open ground, I seemed to move simultaneously from one region of the mind to another, from the concrete to the abstract, from enjoying the profuse expression of mineral, plant, and animal life to contemplating their simple and miraculous interdependency.

And one morning, climbing over rocky wastes with scattered, stunted vegetation until the path became a faint line holding precariously to the face of the final summit, I began to sense a harmony and a unity in life I had never known.

I reached the summit as the cold air became alive with the growing and melting geography of the skies. At the horizon, where the sun would appear, was a great formation of burning silver like a range of unbelievably magnificent mountains, with scarlet-flaming crags; and higher, shifting contours in the deepening light, was a string of ice-pale green lakes, lost among masses of white gold and violet and fire-red. The remainder of the heavens was a vast multi-colored ocean in which islands and continents floated and blazed briefly before fading to embers and ashes.

Then the sun arose, and blue began to drown the dawn colors. I closed my eyes and, aware of a new sense of dedication, breathed an invocation. Something was within the grasp of experience, as near and as elusive as light itself. An energy more subtle than light was streaming through all things, giving sustenance. A moment came when a sudden inflowing of love, of steadily heightening vibration, thrust the center of consciousness upward beyond thought, beyond self, into a radiant realm where, infinitely deeply, white flame spanned opposite shores, fused individualized being and universal being through a bridge of streaming fire.

Life, at that moment, became known as a path of return through service, and the world of appearances was seen as a field of transient fragments behind which, synthesizing all that is, dwells One Supreme Life manifesting itself eternally. And there was within me a seed of this Spirit, a seed which could be nourished only in the carefully prepared ground of consciousness; and this divinity alone was the imperishable essence of man, the energic source like an inner sun to his life.

Afterwards I stood there in a kind of joyous transfixion, somewhat surprised and relieved to see that no angel choir had appeared in the skies, no stream burst out of the mountain, nor had any visible change at all occurred in the world, except the change in me. And that change was signaled by a rush of ideas that revised every attitude and opinion I had ever had, until an hour or so later, feeling like an instrument equipped to handle small voltage that had been struck by lightning instead, I returned slowly to the village.

8. ASPECTS OF THE
ASCETIC WAY

1. TOWARD A SANE ASCETICISM

Once, when the Buddha discovered his follower Sona endangering his health by practicing austerities, he asked:

"What do you think of this, Sona? Were you clever at playing the stringed music of the lute when formerly you were a householder?"

"Yes, Lord."

"What do you think of this, Sona? When the strings of your lute were too taut, was your lute at that time tuneful and fit to play?"

"No, indeed, Lord."

"What do you think of this, Sona? When the strings of

your lute were too slack, was your lute at that time tuneful
and fit to play?"

"No, indeed, Lord."

"What do you think of this, Sona? When the strings of
your lute were neither too taut nor too slack, but were
keyed to an even pitch, was your lute at that time tuneful
and fit to play?"

"Yes, Lord."

"Even so, Sona, too much exercise of energy conduces to
restlessness, and too little exercise of energy conduces to
slothfulness. Therefore, Sona, determine upon evenness in
energy and evenness of faculties."

The advice—Christian, Muslim, and Hindu saints would
agree—is sound. But they would also agree that, at one stage
of the spiritual life, such counsel is exceedingly difficult to
follow.

What, then, is the background of the drive towards asceticism? What basis has the drive? And how can we achieve
a sane asceticism?

There are two great stages of the spiritual life.

The first is called by such names as the Path of Purification, the Path of Probation, and the Purgative Way. This
stage is a preparation of the personality for higher realization. Its key is that only the pure in heart can see or know
God. It consists of a negative aspect—the elimination of
qualities of being and behavior which are incompatible with
the selfless love-wisdom of the soul; and a positive aspect—
the deliberate effort to discipline the lower self into the
closest possible resemblance to the spiritual self.

The second stage is described by such terms as the Path

of Enlightenment, the Path of Discipleship, and the Unitive Way. This stage is marked by a degree of consecration and enlightenment from which there is no turning away from God and back to a materialistic life. It also consists of two parts: first, full awareness of oneself as the spiritual self in relation to God or the Absolute; and second, the ultimate stage of consciousness in which all relationships are resolved and God-nature alone remains experiencing itself.

It is the first stage of the Way, and especially in its negative aspect, that tempts us to ascetic extremes. A point is reached when the dominant desire of the personality is for God; yet other desires remain, deeply embedded in mind and habit, and obstruct the fulfillment of the God-desire. We begin to recognize that further progress depends on the elimination of these personality obstructions. Desire, emotion, and mind must be controlled.

Eckhart, ever the even-minded teacher-saint, describes the goal of the Purgative Way in reply to the question, what is purity? "It is that a man should have turned himself away from all creatures and have set his heart so entirely on the Pure Good that no creature is to him a comfort, that he has no desire for anything creaturely, save so far as he may apprehend therein the Pure Good, which is God. And as little as the bright eye can endure anything foreign in it, so little can the pure soul bear anything in it, any stain on it, that comes between it and God. To it all creatures are pure to enjoy; for it enjoys all creatures in God, and God in all creatures."

The very intensity of our effort is apt to betray us. The obstacles must be removed at any cost and nothing else matters, so that our whole personality effort becomes focused on subjugating the lower nature to conform with the ideal. The great danger at this time is that our concern with practicing intelligent love may be replaced by the devastating use of personal will only. This may be complicated by a growing guilt complex, by a sense of sinfulness and the need to suffer and do penance in order to pay off one's debt of sin or bad *karma*. The obsession with one's weaknesses may also lead to an unhealthy contempt for the body, its needs being often treated as unnecessary desires. In short, the disciplinary emphasis shifts from the creative release of innate spiritual qualities to the destruction of obstructing qualities and habits; and instead of developing the intelligent love which makes our vices obsolete, we intensify the personal will considered necessary to defeat the enemy within.

What workable attitude can we formulate to guide us towards a sane asceticism?

We need to remember that each of us has different spiritual needs at different times. Our needs as beginners are very unlike our needs at a later stage. And the needs of two individuals, at the same stage of development, may also differ, according to temperament, physical make-up, abilities, problems, and other factors. Right timing is often the critical element in determining whether we succeed or fail in our disciplines.

Certainly the saints of every religion would agree with the spirit of this ancient Hindu injunction: "One must surrender his ego for the sake of the family, his family for the sake of the country, his country for the sake of the world, and everything for the sake of God." Yet I know of many ashramas and monasteries which regularly turn away seemingly dedicated young men and women; their "time has not yet come," often because they have left behind them serious and rightful duties still unfinished. "Be ye therefore perfect," Jesus declares in the Sermon on the Mount, "even as your Father which is in heaven is perfect." But instead of seeking the whole of perfection at once, we are wiser to work for perfection stage by stage.

We need to remember, second, that our master motive in all spiritual effort is to seek self-fulfillment with intelligent love, in order to be of greater service to others. Our primary responsibility is to perfect our own little self-world; in doing this we must not let our zeal lead us to become self-appointed architects of the lives of others. One must cease to be a perfectionist where others are concerned; one must be a perfectionist for himself alone.

We must be wisely aware of the impact of our example on others. We should try to live inoffensively and unobtrusively. Showy extremes of self-mortification benefit no one. The true ascetic is never publicly known as such, though he be your next-door neighbor. Moreover, it is also true that certain socially accepted practices, such as drinking, may be harmless enough as a spiritual individual would follow them; yet if any of these practices are potentially harmful to others he might avoid them because of the influence of his example on others. Intelligent love requires us to avoid wrong-doing and also any seeming appearance of it.

And we need to remember, finally, that as consciousness

expands numerous problems simply evaporate. This is especially so with all the problems which creep forth from wrong desire. Sane ascetic practices are designed to bring these under control. When right desire becomes automatic we concentrate increasingly on God's will in and through us. It is also true that some problems painfully and wrongfully but ultimately eliminate themselves through satiety, through repulsion from the once attractive objects of desire. But the best method of outgrowing personality problems is to attain a level of consciousness and a refinement of being where the problems can no longer exist.

By keeping these few points in mind we can avoid ascetic excesses. We can speed up the work of self-purification. By maintaining an evenness in energy and evenness of faculties, a common sense balance of being, we can step more quickly from the Path of Purification onto the Path of Enlightenment.

2. THE VOW OF POVERTY

Poverty has its advantages. Milarepa, the great Tibetan saint of the eleventh and twelfth centuries, records: "One night a person, believing that I possessed some wealth, came and, groping about, stealthily pried into every corner of my cave. Upon my observing this, I laughed outright and said, 'Try if thou canst find anything by night where I have failed by daylight.' The person himself could not help laughing, too; and then he went away."

Poverty is of two kinds: absence of physical possessions; and nonattachment. In monastic practice the first is followed to help to attain the second. Yet, even with the first, some sleight-of-mind often seems to be involved. What does it matter whether or not you own food, shelter, clothing, and other necessities, as long as these are always available when you need them? Not long ago I heard of a family man, a man fairly new to the spiritual life, who prides himself on having taken a vow of actual poverty. His system is simple: he gives everything, including his salary, to his wife and she makes him a gift of whatever he needs. The way of the wandering monk or sadhu seems closest to the spirit of the vow of poverty, yet even his way of life is dependent on those who do not forego possessions. Clearly the vow of physical poverty is not a principle practical for universal adoption.

The real intent of spiritual poverty, of being "poor in spirit," is indicated in a Tibetan precept: "To have but few desires and satisfaction with simple things is the sign of a superior man." This state, as we read in II Corinthians, is that of "having nothing, and yet possessing all things." As our desire to know God or reality increases, pushing aside other desires, we give up more and more because we need less and less. The more strongly we crave God-knowledge the more indifferent we become to other things, to material possessions, to emotional attachments, to nonspiritual intellectual interests. Our whole compulsion becomes not to acquire possessions but to share them or to give them away, and to act according to Jesus' counsel: "Lay up for yourselves treasures in heaven, where neither moth nor rust doth corrupt, and where thieves do not break through nor steal: for where your treasure is, there will your heart be also."

The vow of physical poverty was never meant for the householder. It would violate the most fundamental principles if a married man gave away his home and all possessions and refused to work for money and left his wife and children to shift for themselves. Swami Vivekananda describes the true duties of the householder thus: "The householder who struggles to get rich by good means and for good purposes is doing practically the same thing for the attainment of his salvation as the anchorite in his cell, who is praying; for in that we see in him only a different aspect of the self-same virtues of self-surrender and self-sacrifice, prompted by feelings of devotion to God and to all that is His." The essential requirement of poverty is nonattachment, and it is this that married people are urged to seek. As the *Maha-Nirvana-Tantra* declares, "The householder should be devoted to God; realization of God in and through everything should be his life goal. He must work constantly and perform all his duties; and the fruits of whatever he does he must give up to God."

Once more, then, we have the question of right motivation, the need to interpret nonattachment in terms of intelligent love. Good and evil are not innate in money and property, but in one's motive in acquiring and using them. All we need to do is to redeem money and possessions by using them wisely to serve others. I know a man who very deliberately attempts to earn all the wealth he possibly can, so that he will have more to give away; and to my mind he is one of the saintliest persons I have ever known. And once I knew a minister who greedily hoarded every cent that came his way, so that he might have, as he put it, "the peace of mind that comes with financial security"; and it seems to me he was one of the most subtly selfish persons I have ever known.

The danger is to accumulate wealth and not to share it. The excess, spiritual teachers say, ought to be skimmed off constantly. As Kabir declares: "When there is an excess of water in the boat or of money in the home, the wise use both hands to throw it out." By doing this the householder has a chance to keep his treasure and his heart where they belong, in the Kingdom of God.

A last thought on what seems to be a highly erroneous misapplication of the poverty theme. We often hear religiously inclined people dissertate on the abominations of "mechanized life" and bewail the passing of "the simple life." They appear to find every mechanical contraption an insurmountable obstruction to spiritual achievement. Their way to heaven seems to be blocked by an obstacle course of automobiles, television sets, telephones, iceboxes, dishwashers, vacuum cleaners, and what-have-you. Such time-saving appliances, I believe, are among the many happy blessings we have. Time once demanded for drudgery can now be given to creative pursuits. The only question here is in how to spend these reclaimed hours: are they to be spent cursing the appliances which have given us the leisure to indulge in cursing?

3. "WHATEVER YOU DO, DON'T GET A CAT!"

Once I heard a guru laughingly warn a young disciple who was about to retire to a solitary place for several months of meditation and study: "Whatever you do, don't get a cat!"

When I inquired what his cryptic remark meant, he told me an old story which illustrates the necessity of nonattachment. A young monk, possessing only a water jug and the thread-bare garments he wore, entered a lonely forest to meditate. All went well for a few days, except that at night mice came to gnaw at his clothes. So, to protect his clothing, the monk went to a village and procured a cat. All went well for a few weeks, except that the cat was accustomed to milk and howled every time it had to drink water instead. So the monk arranged to have a cow. All went well for a few months, except that the cow required better pasturage. So the monk got a farm hand to clear a pasture and to care for the cow. All went well, except that the farm hand got lonely and brought his family to live with him. So the monk and the farm hand constructed a suitable farmhouse. All went well, except that farm and household affairs became too time-consuming. So the monk invited a talented girl who was a distant cousin to come to help him. All went well, except that the girl soon thought that, since they lived in the same house, perhaps it would be better for them to get married . . . And one day the former monk, now white-haired, was approached for advice by one of his grandsons who was about to become a monk. And the old man, musing over the problem, suddenly remembered his own past and sat bolt upright. "Whatever you do," he said fervently, "don't get a cat!"

4. ON BEGGING

Some conformance with what society expects of its holy men is sometimes desirable. Once there was a humble sadhu whose spiritual disciplines were being seriously distracted by his near-starvation diet. After due meditation on his problem, he gave away his beloved little beggar's bowl and obtained a much larger pot. Several weeks later he was visited by a fellow sadhu who at once exclaimed in astonishment at his friend's sleek well-fed appearance. The little sadhu shook his head with sad wisdom. "Since obtaining the new pot," he explained, "I am showered with food by everyone. The big pot, you see, makes them think I am an *important* beggar."

5. FOOD, FASTS, AND SPECIAL DIETS

Cicero's advice seems as sound today as ever: "Thou shouldst eat to live; not live to eat." We need wholesome food for good health; and we should want only what we need. Gluttony is one of the seven deadly sins because it eventually destroys health and, worse, all else is liable to be shoved aside in the effort to achieve maximum sensory satisfaction. But food appears to be a problem for many aspirants when, in their abundance, they suddenly feel guilt-stricken by the knowledge that many people on earth are suffering from malnutrition and some are dying of starvation.

Here enters one of the two reasons, I believe, why periodic fasting is desirable. The first reason, which you can test for yourself, is that sanely limited fasting heightens one's spiritual sensitivity: to understand this, think of how loggy you feel and how unresponsive your mind is after heavy eating. Moreover, fasting can help you develop loving understanding and compassion for the needy if, while you fast, you identify yourself vicariously with their suffering. And it can give you a technique of direct action for eliminating a sense of guilt and sharing your plenty with those in need. When you fast, why not estimate the cost of the meals you might have had and donate that amount to an organization serving the underfed?

There are several types of commonly practiced fasts (all permit the taking of water): from one evening through the next day until the next morning, observed once or twice a month; from sunrise to sunset, which may be practiced weekly, biweekly, or monthly; all-day fasting on a holy day or, sometimes, on an all-day spiritual retreat. Many religions have special practices, of course: for example, some require a period of fasting before participating in certain religious ceremonies. The all-day fast, once or twice monthly, is a reasonable practice for most aspirants, assuming, naturally, one's health would not be harmfully affected. But moderation should be the key. St. François de Sales, a biographer reports, "used to say that the spirit could not endure the body when overfed, but that, if underfed, the body could not endure the spirit." If this truth is understood, one can benefit from fasting.

One of the most controversial of all questions about religious practices is that of special diets. There are five chief schools of opinion:

Eat any wholesome food you like, but eat moderately. Most Christians subscribe to this.

Exclude certain meats. Orthodox Jews and Muslims abstain from eating pork.

Exclude all meat except sea food and/or fowl (eggs may or

may not be included). Certain Hindu groups belong to this category.

Exclude all meat (eggs may or may not be included, and some groups distinguish between fertilized and unfertilized eggs, permitting consumption of the latter). Some Hindus, and vegetarians in general, follow this diet.

Exclude all meat and certain vegetables. Orthodox Jains refuse vegetables which grow underground; and some religious groups also forbid vegetables (such as onions) which are believed to contribute to sexual excitement.

Arguments for and against these various diets, as well as for numerous less well-known diets, are practically endless. This fact remains, however: Christian saints have achieved divine union on diets which included meat. Jewish and Muslim saints have attained God-realization on pork-free diets. Buddhist saints have experienced *sunyata* on diets which, for some, included meat, and for others, excluded meat. Hindu saints have achieved *samadhi* on vegetarian diets, and also diets which allowed seafood and, sometimes, fowl. Jain saints have found liberation on their own special diet.

If we accept this inescapable evidence, we can formulate a simple rule for determining diet. Follow any diet which you are convinced is right and which raises no sense of obstruction to spiritual fulfillment. And never let disagreement with the diets of others become itself an obstacle.

6. THE PROBLEM OF ALCOHOL

How dangerous is a glass of wine or a cocktail? Is having an alcoholic drink morally right or wrong?

One sweet old lady I once knew was dead set against the "evils of drink," yet every night before retiring, for her "health's sake," had a stiff dose of a patent-medicine "spring tonic" which was about twice as strongly laced with alcohol as an average wine. And I heard of an elderly gentleman who, for undivulged reasons of his own, was waging a relentless letters-to-the-editor campaign to make it a capital offense to manufacture, handle, or use alcoholic beverages. These are mild examples, I think, of extreme attitudes towards alcohol which are constantly clashing.

Let us recognize first that there is nothing innately evil in alcohol itself. Like a gun, all depends on how we use it; and this is where morality appears. Many medicines contain alcohol, and few or no people object. In one of the most sacred rites of the Christian faith, many churches utilize wine. In Christendom, at least, some monasteries have traditionally derived part or all of their income from the production of wines and liqueurs; Christian monks have explained this by citing the miracle of the wedding feast, when Jesus turned water into wine, and by quoting from I Timothy, "use a little wine for thy stomach's sake." [1]

The chief dangers of drinking, it seems generally agreed, arise from excess, when the need for a drink turns into an unbreakable and vicious habit. Then alcohol becomes a misty avenue of escape from everyday realities. In many cases it drains off money desperately needed by one's family. With a far-gone alcoholic it produces permanent physical damage,

---

[1] Once, when I mentioned Jesus' miracle to an old Buddhist monk, he replied thoughtfully: "But would it not have been better had this Great One turned all the wine into water?"

especially to brain tissue, inhibitions are destroyed, and actions may range from the foolish to the criminally insane. Because of these dangers from excessive drinking, and because for some people alcohol is habit-forming from the start, spiritual leaders of every religion refuse general approval to drinking.

A spiritual approach to the problem might proceed as follows.

First, let us recognize that every serious aspirant must be in full conscious control of all his faculties during his waking hours. This immediately rules out any except possibly light use of alcohol.

Second, let us ask whether one has sufficient self-control to keep the practice from becoming habit-forming?

Third, if one decides to drink lightly, let us inquire what his motive for drinking is, and would he find this motive spiritually acceptable? Further, would he be unmistakably certain that such use of alcohol would be spiritually harmless to himself and others? This involves weighing the possible effect of his example on others.

In discussing this problem with leaders of every major religion, I can find unanimous agreement only on these points: anything which impairs the efficiency of an aspirant is bad, and alcohol may easily and quickly do this; the use of alcohol for some becomes excessive, habit-forming, and dangerous to the total state of being. Therefore no general endorsement of drinking can be given. Some leaders, notably Buddhists and Muslims, are opposed to all alcoholic drinks, medicinal use of alcohol being usually excepted, because of specific precepts of their religion. Some are opposed for more personal reasons, such as the belief that the price is a misuse of money better spent, or because of the fear that any exceptions to the rule would be misinterpreted as more general approval. Some oppose "strong drink" but see no harm in the occasional judicious use of light wines, beers, and ales. And some believe that for temperate, mature, and self-controlled individuals, cocktails, highballs, and other drinks are permissible in moderate quantity, provided one's motive and one's action consequent to drinking are spiritually harmless.

Thus the final decision must be referred back to each aspirant. If he is still uncertain after considering all the evidence, he might try testing the position of nonattachment, where he "can take it or leave it." Usually he leaves it.

7. NOTES ON SEX

The sexual act has specific meaning only in the moral context of a particular individual. In this self-context it may signify love or lust, sinfulness or goodness, ugliness or beauty. If it expresses selflessness, if it neither obstructs one's spiritual development nor causes harm to others, then sex can mean love, goodness, and beauty; it can mean the mystery and the miracle by which man perpetuates his kind. If it expresses selfishness, if sex releases a carnal desire that corrupts the self and causes suffering to others, then it is infested with lust, sinfulness, and ugliness; it signifies that one's sense of humanity is lost and that one has moved further away from identity with others and God.

The sexual act, as a gift of love for a life-partner and as a means of assuring the continuity of the race, is not inconsonant with the early and middle stages of spiritual discipline. Ultimately, however, according to the masters of spiritual teaching, celibacy must be embraced. Like every bodily energy, sexual energy must be transmuted; it must be utilized as a part of one's total energy to achieve union between the lower self and the higher self, the spiritual man and God. When God's love is steadily centered in one's God-nature, one has illimitable love to express with perfect impartiality towards all.

Beyond the sexual act itself, the sexual instinct has the power to impart happiness and unhappiness in other areas of human relations. Even without the consummation of the wish in actuality, the effect on one's character may be similar to that which the act might have imprinted. To look on another person with lust, Jesus declares, affects one "in his heart" just as though adultery had actually been committed. However, to look on another person with intelligent love, and as a soul to be served, strengthens the inner purity which assures true happiness for oneself and others.

One essential technique for the control of sexual desire is taught by every religion. The technique is never to let the mind be free. One tries never to allow his attention to fix on and to become attached to any object harmful to himself or others. One saturates his consciousness with spiritual matters, until the mind has no time for other things, so that even the subconscious mind is spiritualized. One avoids, as diligently as possible, everybody and everything reminding him of a wrong outlook on sex. One treats members of the opposite sex, and also his own, as spiritual beings impressed in a body, and one's primary concern becomes aiding others to liberate this divine self. One fixedly practices recognition of the presence of God in himself and others.

8.   CONSIDERATION FOR WOMEN

Naturally the way the average man shows his respect for women varies somewhat from society to society. When a policeman was asked before an inquiry committee in the Indian Punjab why women demonstrators were dragged by their hair, he replied indignantly: "Because we should not touch their bodies."

9. NONVIOLENCE AND DETACHMENT

1. VIOLENCE IN NATURE AND MAN

From the fragrant green profusion of the valley, three of us had climbed—on ponies as far as possible then on foot —to the rocky gray barrenness of 15,000 feet. Resting in the thin air of the summit, we gazed back at the line of our precipitous ascent, and around at the awesome ranges of frozen white towers glinting against the dark blue sky.

When you have reached such a solitary mountaintop, silent except for the whistling of wind against stone, you are likely to feel the purity of the peaks, their aloofness from the human conflict below; you feel the vastness and the wonder of creation, and something within you which communes with something without; yet you are also likely to sense the violence of nature, of the forces which cast up the mountains and the forces which work to bring them down.

One of my companions, a European, commented on these forces. He remarked how energies of comparable intensity act upon human life, shaping or shattering it as physical forces affect the mountains. But there was perplexity in his voice. "Why," he asked, "is there need for violence, in nature or man?"

Our companion, an Indian friend, replied thoughtfully: "Would you like to hear a story—one of the Hindu versions of the creation of the universe?" We nodded, made curious, and he began.

"The Absolute, Brahman, first manifested in form as Brahma, the Creator. And Brahma, in deepest meditation, began to dream of beauty. When He had perfected His dreams, He willed that the beauty should move from thought into form. As He wished, it happened. And the world was without flaw. For a time too great to measure Brahma contemplated the universe, but at last he began to feel dissatisfied. Because it was an unchanging world, and utterly still, without any motion at all, not like Himself, but, for all its beauty, like a corpse. Then Brahma worried. He was unable to solve the problem. He could not destroy the world to make another because he was a Creator only. Then the All-Wise Absolute acted again, sending Shiva the Destroyer and Vishnu the Preserver. Now there could be both creation and destruction and a balancing force between. Then, suddenly, the world was no longer like a corpse—it came alive, it moved. Each part, however small or great, was filled with a life of its own, and also the seed of death. So the world as we know it came into being, because without motion there is no life, and motion is impossible without the meeting of opposing forces.

"But the violence, we would say, has to do only with the disbalance of the world of form. It is our aspect of form that experiences violence and death. And it is said that, through spiritual discipline, we can get beyond violence and death, beyond ignorance and illusion—we can know that the atman, or soul, is of the same deathless essence as the Absolute . . ."

2.   THE SAINTLY ART OF NONVIOLENCE

Sooner or later every sincerely religious person has to come to terms with the problem of nonviolence; then to grapple with it, in himself and society, for the rest of his life.

The injunction to practice nonviolence is, in most religions, a categorical imperative. The *Vedas* command: "Do not injure any being." And the *Dhammapada:* "All men tremble at punishment, all men fear death; remember you are like unto them, and do not kill, nor cause slaughter." And the Bible: "Thou shalt not kill." But the commandment goes further: in Jesus' words, "Love your enemies, bless them that curse you, do good to them that hate you, and pray for them which despitefully use you, and persecute you."

Many people argue, there must be exceptions to the practice of nonviolence. Is one not justified in defending himself from an unfair attack? Or in protecting the innocent and the helpless from assault? Or in discouraging crime by asking the death penalty for the worst criminals? Or, in defense of his home and loved ones, to kill intruders if necessary? Or, if one's country is attacked, to support its war effort?

But another question has to precede these. What *is* non-violence?

True nonviolence is essentially the expression of love-wisdom in its aspect of spiritual harmlessness. Nonviolence is a negative way of looking up from the lower self to a positive attribute of the higher or spiritual self. One loves wisely, wishing well to all, serving the greatest good of all, because, through the God-nature common to all, one is identified with all. Then loving one's neighbor as oneself ceases to be a law or an ideal, but is simply a spontaneously expressed fact of being.

But nonviolence, as a virtue to be developed through successive stages of consciousness, has other meanings for us first. It must reflect one's growing moral strength, and not be used as a defense to conceal faintness of heart. It is one thing for a lion to refrain from attacking a rabbit; another, for a rabbit to refrain from attacking a lion. "Buddha gave up his throne and renounced his position—that was true renunciation," Swami Vivekananda declares. "But can there be any question of renunciation in the case of a beggar who has nothing to renounce?" Gandhi repeatedly warned his followers not to hide behind the concept of *ahimsa*,[1] or nonviolence, but to develop the spiritual force which alone could make its effective practice possible. "Observance of ahimsa is heroism of the highest type," he observed on one occasion, "with no room therein for cowardice or weakness."

[1] One of the five cardinal virtues of Hinduism: purity, self-control, detachment, truth, and nonviolence.

Does this imply that one can practice nonviolence in its early stages without fear? Not at all. In fact, fear even has a role in the development of nonviolence. As Gesell the psychologist observes: "Fear and fortitude are opposites but both are necessary for the growth of character. The full development of fortitude depends upon the experiencing and overcoming of fear. Wholesome fear generates its own mental antibodies. Fear is anticipatory pain. Its antibody is fortitude, the capacity to endure and cope with pain." The self-preservation instinct gives rise to the fear of death, and this fear may represent a perfectly reasonable concern for one's safety or a morbid or cowardly preoccupation with oneself which excludes every consideration except personal safety at any cost. The fear of death is finally eliminated in a healthy spiritual manner when one realizes that the essential self, the spiritual self, is eternally deathless.

The third point is that the practice of nonviolence must be inspired by the motive of intelligent love, which also means dedication to the acquisition and demonstration of truth. To express spiritual harmlessness in the most adverse circumstances requires the soul strength and the absolute fearlessness which come only with great love and the spirit of wise self-sacrifice. If a man has this kind of nonviolence, he has the power to strike; his strength is soul power at its full, constrained; and having the capacity to strike or not, he refrains—not out of fear but wholly because of love. And he is not only able to withhold his blows, be they physical or verbal, but to turn his other cheek for further blows, and to bless his enemies.

On first thought such behavior, in some circumstances,

might seem suicidal, or at least foolhardy. But many subtleties in the observance of nonviolence are involved here. Indian gurus, for instance, like to tell this tale about the practice of nonviolence. A ferocious king cobra, which had terrorized the cowherds of a village and prevented them from grazing their cows in a desirable meadow, was persuaded by a sadhu to take a vow of nonviolence and, in fact, to meditate daily on God's name. Some months later, when the sadhu returned to the meadow, he discovered the snake in very bad shape. The baffled and sorrowful cobra explained that when he had attempted to make friends with the cowherds, and they had learned he was now harmless, they had beaten him with sticks and stones and left him for dead. "Revered sir," the cobra begged, "pray tell me where I have gone wrong." "My poor friend!" the sadhu exclaimed pityingly. "I said you must not bite—not that you were forbidden to hiss as loudly as you like!"

This is one factor—the right to show spiritual force judiciously, if one's motive is love. The classic illustration of this is Jesus casting the moneylenders out of the temple. This is not righteous indignation (which the saints deplore, never feeling either righteous or indignant), but the inexorable outflowing of a spiritual force wishing the ultimate highest good of every creature. Another aspect of that fearless and open love is often, to a considerable extent, its own protection. Unlike hatred, which attacks, destroys, and seeks death, love protects, creates, and seeks life. The nonviolent person carries out the deep-rooted will in everyone to live, to extend relationships; and he expresses the love force by which this may be accomplished, by which parts may be combined in a whole, all men in the Life of God. And frequently his opponents will respond to this power of love-wisdom. Enmity, we know, is hardly likely to cease when met by hatred; it is most apt to disappear in the presence of perfect nonviolence. And a third factor, frequently mentioned by the saints, is the protection afforded to one who has complete trust in God. Allied with this is the power of prayer and meditation. This gives a strength, Gandhi says, which "comes from the belief that God sits in the hearts of all and that there should be no fear in the presence of God. The knowledge of the omnipresence of God also means respect for the lives even of those who may be called opponents." And he utters the poignant words: "Mankind would die if there were no exhibition any time and anywhere of the divine in man."

The aspirant should practice nonviolence to the maximum of his ability. But we may as well acknowledge frankly that the beginner, if suddenly confronted by violence, is less capable than the experienced disciple of evoking the spiritual force needed to resist retaliation in violence. And we need to remember that the householder has others who are dependent upon him, while the monk normally does not. There is little question as to what constitutes right action for the aspirant who is also a monk, because he will have taken a vow of nonviolence. Still, the situation is more complicated for the enlightened disciple who is also a householder.

If their most consecrated efforts to assure nonviolence have failed, the lay aspirant and the householder are, I believe, justified to use force as a last resort in order to protect themselves and others from an unprovoked physical attack. However, their motive must be intelligent love; they should attempt not to injure, but to prevent injury; they should act not only to defend themselves or others, but to mitigate the degree of criminality intended by the attacker; and at every moment they should strive to make clear their lack of malice and their spirit of love. The practice of nonviolence is not meant to produce unnecessary or foolish martyrs, but to release as much of the healing power of love-wisdom as each aspirant or disciple can evoke and manifest. True, it may seem difficult or impossible to fight in a spirit of love, and it is, for the average person. But the dedicated aspirant or disciple has ceased to be average.

The way of the disciple without dependents and the monk requires willingness to die, if necessary, to express the fearless love-wisdom of the God-nature. The enlightened disciple knows that the God-nature in himself is in all, and it is this which he is and which he serves in others. Nonviolence at this level is depicted in an Indian story about a monk who, without warning or provocation and without retaliation, was assaulted by a criminal and beaten almost to death. When his brother monks found him and slowly nursed him back to consciousness, getting him to take a little nourishment, they asked who his attacker was. And in a voice feeble yet gentle with love, the monk whispered: "He who attacked me is the same as he who just now has fed me."

For those who accept "Thou shalt not kill" as a categorical imperative, capital punishment of criminals is itself a crime. The most devious arguments and religion-based apologies mean nothing against this imperative. Life, even of the most brutal criminal, must be honored and preserved. Other and more effective deterrents to crime than the death penalty must be recognized, developed, and applied.

So with war. War is a social catastrophe over which most individuals, as such, have no control. The truly spiritual person is unable to endorse murder simply because it has been projected onto so stupifyingly vast a scale. His best and only course is that taken by many people in recent wars: to volunteer for service which will enable him to save rather than to take life.

There is an application of nonviolence which more immediately concerns us; that is, the verbal attacks we make upon one another. The real starting point for the practice of nonviolence begins with our thoughts of others and in our conversations. Malice, slander, gossip, lies, sarcasm, ridicule: are not these forms of violence which are often more disastrous than physical blows? The spiritual way is to infuse all conscious activity with intelligent love. A point is reached where the opinions of others matter little or not at all: the only approval one cherishes is God's. It is here that we can begin immediately to develop practical skill in practicing nonviolence.

The saintly art of nonviolence is not easily mastered. During his last years Gandhi, a master exponent of nonviolence, declared: "Life is a very complex thing, and truth and nonviolence present problems which often defy analysis and judgment. One discovers truth and the method of applying it, that is, *satyagraha* or soul force, by patient endeavor and silent prayer." For the spiritual person there is no alternative to nonviolence. He would not have it otherwise. He believes deeply with Jesus: "Blessed are the peacemakers: for they shall be called the children of God. Blessed are they which

are persecuted for righteousness' sake: for theirs is the kingdom of heaven." He works as a peacemaker to establish this
kingdom here and now on earth.

3. ON WRONG SPEECH

When a follower asked Mohammed for advice after
slandering an acquaintance, he was directed to place a feather
before every door in the community and to come back the
next morning. Upon the man's return, Mohammed suggested,
"Go now and gather the feathers." The man objected. "But
that is impossible! The wind that blew last night scattered
the feathers beyond finding." "Exactly," Mohammed replied. "And thus it is with the wrong words you uttered
against your neighbor."

4. DO NOT LIKE, DO NOT DISLIKE;
ALL WILL THEN BE CLEAR

We look at a simple object, such as a leaf, and at once
we register an opinion, showing pleasure or displeasure with
its shape, color, texture, odor, condition, kind, and so on;
we transform the leaf from what it is in itself to what we
feel and think about it. We call other objects "pleasant" or
"unpleasant," but their pleasantness or unpleasantness exists
only in our opinion. How much more involved is our reaction to another person's appearance, speech, attitudes, ges-
tures, actions, quality of being. How easily we let our emotions and prejudices create a false image of another person,
rather than accepting him as he truly is! And how quickly
we forget that when we find others "irritating," it means
only that we ourselves are irritable!

When we become critical we destroy objectivity. We erect a barrier to understanding. When we consider only what someone's actions mean to us in terms of our own pain or pleasure, we lose touch with his innate nature and needs. We create a conception of him colored by our emotions and thoughts. This prejudiced picture distorts and veils our insight.

Like a mountain lake which reflects in its still waters a majestic snowy peak, our emotional nature has to be made tranquil in order to mirror only the qualities of the spiritual self. Our emotions must reflect only love-wisdom and such qualities as compassion and equanimity which are derived from it.

True knowledge, like true love, is always positive and non-condemnatory. The mind itself then must also be controlled, must be made to give up its embedded habit of criticism, of annihilation through analysis, its destruction of the whole to savor the parts.

The ideal condition of consciousness is expressed in these lines by the Chinese Buddhist patriarch Seng Ts'an (about 600 A.D.):

> The Perfect Way is difficult only for those who pick and choose;
> Do not like, do not dislike; all will then be clear.
> Make a hairbreadth difference, and Heaven and Earth are set apart;
> If you want the truth to stand clear before you, never be for or against.
> The struggle between "for" and "against" is the mind's worst disease . . .

What, then, is the consequence of such spiritual objectivity?

There comes, at first usually through meditation, a stage of realization in which love and knowledge are perfected by fusion in a quality which is more than the sum of the two. At this stage love-wisdom consists of a twofold experience. First, we project a relationship of otherness toward God. Then, in the moment we cease to be the "self," when the divine ceases to be apart from us, when only One remains, that otherness has been destroyed in the experience of perfect identification.

As long as we are attracted to certain objects and repelled by others, personal desire will continue to create obstacles to clear insight. But when we are able to act without acting, to be inwardly as still as the unmoving axle of a revolving wheel, we are able then to advance beyond duality. Neither liking nor disliking, neither being for nor against, we are able to seek the state beyond illumination, when we are no longer that which is illuminated but That which illuminates.[2]

5.   DHRUVA AND THE WHITE ANTS

One of the Indian exemplars of steadfast detachment was the saint Dhruva, who gave up claim to his father's throne to become an ascetic. It is said that his meditative absorption in God was so prolonged and so complete that once, un-

---

[2] In the threefold man (personality, soul, spirit), soul is often referred to in terms of light, while spirit may be described as lightless or even as being dark. Spirit, as the ultimate source of light, is in itself experienced as without light, in the same way that the eye which sees outer events cannot see itself.

known to him, while he meditated white ants constructed an anthill around his motionless body!

6.   ATTAINING TO TRANQUILLITY

Sri Krishna says in the *Bhagavad-Gita* that "the self-controlled man, moving among objects with senses under restraint, and free from attraction and aversion, attains to tranquillity." I believe it is this having the "senses under restraint" that explains best why the detached person is sometimes accused of aloofness or coolness. The more involved others are, the more apart he seems to be. And yet, because of his detachment, he is usually able to act with more loving wisdom than others, not being blinded to anyone's needs. I recall an account I once heard about a sadhu who found himself, at his prayer hour, caught in the middle of a riot between two political factions. Perceiving that he was unable to stop the fighting, and realizing that the riot thus far had nothing to do with him, he sat down with his back against the trunk of a small tree and began to meditate. By the time he had completed his meditation, the riot was nearly over. Arising then, he noted without surprise that he was the only uninjured person present. Calmly and tenderly, and with his mind still on God, he took care of the wounded.

10. SADHUS AND
PSYCHIC POWERS

1. HOLY MIRACLES IN INDIA

How much truth is there in the sensational accounts about
the strange powers and practices of the holy men of India?

These stories may be considered in five groups (which
sometimes overlap). Let us look at some examples in each
category.

One group consists of such reports as these: a man has stuck
an iron skewer through his cheeks so that it passes between
his upper and lower teeth and makes eating and speaking ex-
tremely difficult . . . another is blind from staring at the
sun while reciting his prayers . . . one has held an arm aloft
for so long that the limb is withered and paralyzed . . . one
has deliberately deafened himself . . . one crawls on hands

and knees to as many pilgrimage places as he can reach in his lifetime . . . one lives in a crude shelter scarcely large enough to contain him, where he has sat for a score of years unspeaking and as motionless as possible . . . one has vowed to possess nothing—not even a loincloth or a beggar's bowl —and lives alone in an isolated part of a jungle . . . one, who also lives in isolation, has horribly disfigured himself.

In a second category are these stories: one man is able at will to slow his blood circulation and, for several minutes, to suspend his heartbeat . . . another can survive for weeks beyond the normal point of death by starvation . . . one walks barefooted on blazing coals without being burned . . . this one lives in an unheated cave high in the mountains during months of freezing weather . . . one permits himself to be buried alive in a casket for a week or more at a time . . . one sees distant objects with telescopic clarity . . . one hears sounds which are undetectable to those of ordinary hearing . . . one has incredible strength and, in addition to weight-lifting feats, has slain wild bears and tigers with his bare hands.

In another group are such tales as these: one man, a temple attendant, recites a name of God almost continuously . . . one has devoted all of his adult years to the unceasing and worshipful care of an image of Ganesha . . . another dresses exquisitely in women's clothes and jewelry, uses cosmetics, imitates feminine mannerisms, and regards his relationship to Krishna as that of a bride . . . another gives most of his time to the cultivation of flowers which will be tributes worthy of offering to Lakshmi . . . one smears himself daily at dawn with ashes and cow dung to show his devotion to Shiva . . .

another gives constant loving service, often of the most re-
pugnant and sacrificial nature, to a malicious young whore
whom he serves as his ideal embodiment of the Divine Mother
principle (Shakti) . . . one dances for hours in honor of
Durga until he drops from exhaustion and later resumes his
dancing . . . one, a childless woman, spends her free time
circumambulating a sacred tree while reciting prayers for
fertility.

In a fourth category are these accounts: one is able to identify small articles secretly selected by someone else and concealed from sight in a thick wooden box . . . one can determine accurately, without scientific instruments, where to
drill wells successfully in desert areas . . . another is able
to predict, often months in advance, the exact date and hour
of a person's death . . . one, by the power of his mind only,
can cause an object of light weight to rise into the air . . .
one is able to levitate as high as the great-hall ceiling of a
monastery . . . another can describe correctly, on occasion,
what any of several friends who live in distant places may be
doing at that moment . . . one was seen simultaneously by
friends in two cities several hundred miles apart . . . another is able to kill a bird or small animal and restore it to
life.

A fifth group would include these stories: one, who was
then unknown to a future pupil in England, wrote him suggesting that the two of them concentrate on a single spiritual
thought as a means of resolving a personality clash which was
about to destroy a large nondenominational religious organization, and the plan proved highly successful . . . one,
while walking on a Bengal plain with a group of his disciples,

stepped forward to meet a charging full-grown tiger which suddenly halted, purred as if it were a house cat, and then at his request went peacefully away . . . one healed a young mother of an incurable disease which doctors had declared would be fatal within a year . . . another, through a series of vivid dreams, inspired a European scholar to meet him in a specific Himalayan community for spiritual instruction . . . one was able to evaluate an individual's spiritual state in a few moments, and to make suggestions which were simply expressed and profoundly beneficial . . . another appeared to protect his disciple in an instant of critical psychic danger, and then vanished in the air as mysteriously as he had come . . . another, a Tibetan abbot, good-naturedly proved his reality to a disciple in America with whom he was in telepathic contact by sending his disciple a large bundle of Tibetan incense . . . one, who finds it too time-consuming to penetrate the closed minds of some of his pupils during their waking hours, impresses his most difficult teaching on their minds during their sleeping hours.

You should understand, first of all, that only a few of these stories may be said to represent the norm of religious life in India. The average Indian is as quietly and "normally" devoted to his religion as the average Westerner; it is true, however, that the Indian tends to be more receptive and less critical of tales of wonder than the Occidental. Second, if you have an understanding of Eastern religions, you will appreciate that many practices which seem abnormal to Western eyes either are normal in India or may be recognized as exaggerations of common customs. Third, in the religious history of the West, you will find countless stories comparable to those just given, and many religious customs which are strange and baffling to the orthodox Easterner. Fourth, to gauge the truth of these stories, you would be wise to rely on firsthand experience and documentary evidence. On the hearsay evidence of others you can decide at best only whether or not the evidence seems reasonable in the light of your own experience and reasoning.

Now, with these points in mind, let us examine the stories more closely, to see how many we may be able to accept.

The first group of stories illustrates ascetic extremes. In all the major religions, it is not rare to find aspirants whose excessive zeal leads them to strenuous ascetic practices, from which they usually retreat later to a less self-abusive life. St. Ignatius Loyola is an example. The basic scriptures of Hinduism and Buddhism, as of Christianity, Judaism, and Islam, urge the intelligent practice of ascetic ideals. Most of the members of Hindu and Buddhist monastic orders whom I know and know of, appear to practice asceticism with the same common sense as the monks of other religions. But many sadhus are not members of monastic orders and are not under the control of any religious organization. In fact, anyone who observes some semblance of holy life can call himself a sadhu; which means, to the concern of genuine sadhus, that many incompetents and imposters (often professional beggars) pose as holy men. Cases such as those I have cited perhaps underscore, as much as any social problem, the lack of Indian social services in comparison with those of Western nations, and especially the urgent need of more psychiatrists and mental institutions. Probably most of these extremists, so I have been told by Indian doctors and spiritual leaders, suffer from mental disturbances, such as guilt and Messiah complexes, exhibitionism, and masochism. I have seen many of these extremists, as does anyone who travels in India—and especially in Banaras, where tolerance of them is perhaps greater than anywhere else. In Kalimpong I have seen, for instance, a visiting "holy man" who wore twenty-five or thirty tangerines on his bare chest, back, and arms, by piercing his flesh with the stems.

The accounts in the second category are of superphysical abilities. While specific cases are frequently exaggerations or frauds, there is a substantial basis of truth for many of these reports. Medical and other case histories are available to authenticate an impressive number of them. Many friends whom I regard as trustworthy observers, including doctors, scholars, authors, and religious leaders, have told me of personally witnessing such cases. My own experience has been limited to seeing several unusual but not very remarkable cases.[1] These superphysical abilities as well as certain psychic powers are generally attributed to strenuous yogist training; and in the majority of instances I have been told of, and a few I have witnessed, the possessor was a yogi.[2] These per-

[1] One was the performance of a youthful "Durga dancer." During his twenty-minute dance the boy spent much of his time in a frenzied pouncing up and down upon the red-hot coals of coconut husks. Wincing, I asked one of the boy's friends how the boy did it. "All his life he has never worn shoes," the friend explained. "His father, who was also a dancer, taught him special ways to make the feet tough. The bottom of his feet are maybe as tough as the bottom of your shoes." Afterward, looking at the unharmed soles of the boy's feet, I decided my shoes would have probably finished the dance second best.

[2] Such yogist training is sometimes dangerous—and disastrous. In addition to many cases I know of, I know well three persons (one a European,

formances, however, strike me as being no more difficult or unbelievable than what you can see in any good circus or side show or, in some instances, in a professional magician's exhibition. We often forget, moreover, how little we really understand about our bodily processes and how many latent capacities we have which we never bother to investigate or to develop. It seems hardly necessary to add that these are physical rather than spiritual abilities.

The stories in the third group are easily understandable if you know Hinduism, as examples of devotionalism, some of them going well beyond the norm. The repetitious recitation of a name of God or a brief prayer is common in every religion, but especially so in Hinduism and Mahayana Buddhism. There is the Hindu *japam*; the Buddhist *buddhanusmriti*, *nembutsu*, or *nien-fo*; the Muslim *dhikr*; and the Christian "saying the rosary." Religious objects in all religions are handled with special veneration; and the care of images in most Hindu temples is an outstanding example. Some Hindus regard the image as being one of the dwelling places of the deity or as possessing some of his power. In many temples the images are lovingly cared for—bathed in the morning, offered food and flowers and other gifts during the day, entertained with music and readings, prepared for sleep in the evening. The sadhu who dresses in women's

---

the others Indians) who went insane as the result of wrong instruction or wrong practice in a yoga involving certain exercises affecting the nervous system. (Happily all recovered, which is not always the case.) In Kashmir I became friendly with a young sadhu whose death in a matter of months had been predicted by his doctors. Through a similar yoga he had developed an acute nervous affliction which, while not affecting his mind directly, wracked his body at frequent intervals with a strange type of convulsion.

finery is neither homosexual nor insane, as an uninformed person might hastily conclude, but is following a little-known and exacting yoga. In the literature of many religions the soul is sometimes described as feminine and the Incoming Presence or Spirit as masculine. St. Bernard often calls the soul the bride and Jesus the Bridegroom; Christian nuns frequently are called Brides of Jesus; and the Sufis, in particular, appropriated the terminology of human love to symbolize the experiences of divine love. This sadhu's yoga, which requires him to spend most of his time in devotional practices and meditation, has such implications. Other examples, and numerous stories like them, also may be explained in terms of Hindu devotionalism.

The fourth category of stories concerns psychic and magical abilities. Most of the cases mentioned, and many others of similar nature, are on constantly recurrent themes—some of them, such as levitation,[3] multiple appearance, and restor-

---

[3] Levitation—the ability to lift oneself into the air without visible support or cause—has some staunch exponents in India. Two "explanations" of levitation are usually given: one group contends that a certain yoga produces subtle bodily changes which make the phenomenon possible; the other group, contends the feat is achieved through the cooperation of certain supernatural entities, or "spirits," whose aid is evoked by the proper recitation of certain secret *mantras*. An instance said to have been of the second type has been described to me in detail by one of the two Westerners who witnessed the event; and I have also heard substantially the same description from close friends of two other eyewitnesses. In this incident the levitator, a Tibetan oracle, is reported to have been lifted six or eight feet into the air by his supernatural "friends." The Westerners concerned are unwilling to discuss the matter except privately and will pursue it no further, claiming (rightly, I believe) that the authenticity of the episode can be established in no way except through the dubious means of their own testimony; and one, who is a recognized scholar in Tibetan studies, feels that such testimony would only jeopardize his reputation for serious factual research. As a counterbalance to this story, I

ation of the dead, known to be at least a thousand to a few thousand years old. Most spiritual preceptors regard psychic or so-called occult powers as being of two kinds: the lower, of the personality and the higher, of the spiritual self. Lower psychic powers are considered a definite hazard to spiritual development. They usually lead to self-aggrandizement and a wrong sense of personal power, and have nothing to do with God-realization. Higher psychic powers, which are understood as by-products of spiritual effort and not as the goal of sadhana, are held to be harmless only if not deliberately cultivated and if used rarely and solely for pure spiritual purpose. There is an extensive literature which claims to give proof of instances such as I have described.[4] Serious investigators discount the vast majority of cases on many grounds, ranging from the factor of coincidence, the distortion of stories in retelling, and false testimony, to the gullibility of some witnesses, trickery on the part of some "psychic" performers, and the universal desire of people to believe in the miraculous and the supernatural. But most investigators appear to accept as true a small hard-core number of cases. Moreover, there is another argument for the existence of psychic phenomena, the argument by inference: if such powers did not exist, why would so many of the greatest saints and spiritual teachers have warned their followers of their

---

should mention another. During a discussion with a swami in South India, who is esteemed for his knowledge of psychic powers, I asked, "Have you ever seen anyone levitate?" "Only once," the man replied—"when a brother monk sat in a chair already occupied by a scorpion."

[4] See, for example, Dr. J. B. Rhine's books and articles on investigations of extrasensory perception, publications of The Society for Psychical Research, and publications and reports of The Parapsychology Foundation.

dangers? It will be evident to you, I am sure, that most of the cases mentioned are clearly examples of lower psychism, having little if anything to do with the spiritual life as such.

The final group of stories concerns highly unusual spiritual experiences. Aside from whether or not these specific stories seem true and of spiritual significance, at least the *possibility* of extraordinary or miraculous spiritual experience is admitted by every major religion. Christians, for example, believe events as varied as Jesus' miracles and the miracles worked by his followers, St. Paul's conversion, and the angel who appeared at the sepulcher to speak to the two Marys. Each of the leading religions has such a basis in its scriptures and in the lives of its saints.

These stories were told to me as personal experiences by close and esteemed friends. For example, one is a distinguished Protestant clergyman and author; one is a well-known Hindu scholar whose works have won critical acceptance in both East and West; and another was, for many years, the eminent and beloved leader of a large nondenominational religious organization. These accounts were given to me privately and in full detail, and with the understanding that the names of those concerned would not be revealed. Each witness regarded his experience as intensely personal and deeply spiritual, contending it must never be allowed to become a matter of controversial discussion.

You will appreciate at once, I think, the perplexing problem in discrimination created by the fifth group of stories. I have known the reporters intimately for many years. I have never had cause, even in the least matters, to suspect the integrity of any. Each is wholly dedicated to the spiritual life, and has striven in all things to exemplify his high ideals. Several told me their stories spontaneously in the course of private conversation, while the others recounted their experiences upon my request for information of this kind. None asked me to believe his story, and none tried to convince me of its truth: each communicated his experience for whatever significance it might hold for me. What, then, should our reaction be? Let us not forget that we need to question everything regardless of the authority behind it. I heard these stories from those concerned, with one exception. That exception was an experience of my own, which is one of the examples given. Perhaps, as we ponder the problem of discrimination which this matter raises, we may experience a new and deeper realization of what discrimination is and when and how to apply it. For, in balancing the necessary faith and the honest doubt which are both essential to spiritual growth, one finds there are times to believe, times to disbelieve, and times neither to believe nor to disbelieve.

2. THE SIX AND THE EIGHT OCCULT POWERS

The master teachers of Buddhism and Hinduism alike disparage the pursuit of occult powers. Yet both religions have traditional teachings about the nature of such powers. According to Buddhism, there are six of these powers or *abhijna* (higher knowledges). All are considered without spiritual consequence except the last; however, while representing mundane achievement, these powers may be spiritually significant as means; but only the last is considered in itself to be a transcendental power. The first is the production out of the physical body of a mind-created body which is free from the usual limitations of time and space. With this type of body one is said to be able, for example, to fly unobstructed through solid materials and to move at will, within a twinkling, between distant places. The Bodhisattvas, after discarding the normal physical body, are said to carry on their compassionate service to humanity in such glorified bodies. Other powers are "the divine ear," or clairaudience; mind reading, telepathy; remembrance of former lives; "the divine eye," a special type of clairvoyance; and the last is transcendental insight into the real nature of the phenomenal world. According to Hinduism, there are eight of these powers, *ashta siddhis*. They give one the power to become the smallest of the small, the largest of the large, the heaviest of the heavy, the lightest of the light, and to gain overlordship, to obtain anything and everything at will, to bring things under subjugation, and to be pervasive. Patanjali's *Yoga Aphorisms* describes the nature of these powers and how they may be developed, then recommends that the student leave them strictly alone, as spiritually worthless. Perhaps you will agree that the continuing forcefulness with which these teachings are imparted suggests a genuine need among spiritual aspirants for correct orientation in this field.

3. FIVE STORIES ABOUT PSYCHIC ABILITIES

Indian spiritual preceptors have issued countless warnings to their pupils about the folly and the danger of seeking psychic powers. They can quote many scriptural injunctions, such as Krishna's statement to Arjuna that anyone who possesses such abilities is unable to attain God-realization. They can refer to such great teachers as Patanjali, who warns that such powers bar one from liberation. They can recite true stories of the downfall and sometimes self-destruction of those who have sought such psychic gifts instead of God. But they especially like to drive their points home with a host of simple and pungent stories.

When a guru's young pupil, who had psychic power, missed the ferryboat to his teacher's ashrama, he simply walked across the river rather than wait for the boat to return. Upon his arrival he was met by his guru, who had seen him approaching. "Tell me, my son," the guru requested, "how much the ferry ride costs." "Why," the young man replied, "only the smallest copper coin." "Then that is exactly the amount your gift is worth," the teacher said quietly.

A sadhu who had learned how to fly became more and more obsessed with the thought that he was actually lord of the kingdom of birds. One day, deciding to announce himself to his feathered "subjects" in the Himalayas, he went there and was soon espied by a flock of great eagles. "Who is this creature who mocks us?" the eagles angrily asked each other. Whereupon, even as the sadhu shouted, "I proclaim myself to be your lord!" the eagles fell upon him and quickly destroyed him.

A yogi was meditating beside the sea when a storm arose. Irritated that it interfered with his reflections, he summoned his psychic power and commanded, "Let the storm cease!" Then in a second the sea became glassy quiet, a ship in full sail suddenly capsized, and everybody aboard was drowned. Shiva, seeing this abuse of power, cast the yogi into hell.

A sadhu who had the power to kill animals and then restore them to life was asked by a stranger if he could demonstrate this ability with an elephant. The sadhu, with a mighty effort, managed to do so. Then the stranger asked, "But how has this helped you? Do you feel inspired? Are you now closer to God-realization?" While the abashed sadhu was searching for a reply, the stranger revealed himself to be the Lord and suddenly vanished.

A yogi who had attained so much psychic power that he was able to change life from one form to another, avenged himself by turning an old enemy into a cat in his enemy's household. The Lord, to teach the avenger a lesson, promptly turned the yogi into a mouse in the same household.

11. GURU AND CHELA

I. THE GURU-CHELA RELATIONSHIP

The guru-chela [1] relationship, as it exists in India, is without Western counterpart. The nearest approximation occurs in monasteries and convents, but even there the difference in the relationship of the spiritual counsellor and the acolyte is considerable.

There are numerous surface differences. The Western teacher and his pupils normally live in a well-equipped monastery, while the average Indian teacher has a very small ashrama or no permanent home at all. The Western teacher, who is likely to have a staff of assistants, favors much formal

[1] Guru—spiritual teacher; chela (or *shishya*)—pupil.

147

instruction and the study of books; the Indian teacher, who is typically a one-man school, teaches through conversation and example and may never even possess a book. The Western teacher is responsible to higher church officials for the instruction he imparts; the Indian teacher, while he may have a superior in his own guru or if he belongs to one of a small number of groups, more usually is himself considered the final authority on the appropriateness of what he teaches. The Western teacher is usually a monk; the Indian teacher may be a monk, but generally is a sadhu who has never been associated with a monastery, or a householder who has a wife and children. The Western teacher finds his pupils in his own monastery or among lay pupils attracted to him; the Indian teacher, generally independent of any religious organization, may have monks among his pupils.

There are deeper differences in matters of immediate spiritual goal and of method and technique by which the goal is sought. The Western teacher's foremost object is to try to aid his pupil in securing the forgiveness of his sins and of obtaining a new birth and salvation through grace; the Indian teacher, who deals with sin as ignorance in terms of karma, attempts to lead his pupil to the unitive knowledge of God-realization through self-mastery achieved by experience of immanent divinity. The Western teacher offers a monastic discipline, with its well-ordered round of meditations, prayers, devotional services, confessionals, penances, and often some form of service; the Indian teacher concentrates almost exclusively on imparting the disciplines necessary to practice the yoga for which the pupil seems most inherently suited, and the primary discipline usually consists of long hours of carefully supervised meditation supplemented by devotional exercises, study, and holy pilgrimages, with little emphasis, except in a few sects, on service of a social nature.

But the greatest difference by far, between West and East, is in the very concept of the teacher-pupil relationship. The Western teacher is considered to be helpful but not essential to the pupil's attainment of salvation. The Indian teacher is regarded by most Indians as being an indispensable necessity to one who seriously seeks liberation. The Western teacher holds that ultimately the pupil is a free agent, and is responsible for his own success or failure regardless of the instructor's part. The Indian teacher, when he accepts a pupil, requires a strict obedience from the pupil in all matters; both teacher and pupil believe that, so long as the pupil is faithful to the guru's teaching, the teacher has assumed full karmic responsibility for the pupil. So long as the pupil is faithful, and for the duration of the training, the teacher ultimately must bear the karma produced by the effects of the causes which he has initiated in the pupil's life. The Western teacher is regarded as simply a man, perhaps wiser and more loving than most men. The Indian teacher is never considered by his pupils to be merely a man, but is revered as one through whom divinity of some degree is made manifest. Thus the Eastern guru-chela relationship assumes a depth of significance unknown in the West; it is deemed a sacred bond of inviolable love and trust, based on the acknowledgment of the commingling of their spiritual karmas and destinies.

The ideal relationship between the instructor and the instructed, it seems to me, is a blending of the attitudes of West and East. The instructor must admit the free will of the instructed, and the pupil's right at all times to act according to his highest spiritual insight; but, at the same time, if the pupil is unwilling to abide exactly by the teacher's instruction, the teacher cannot be considered responsible for any consequent ill effects. Therefore, both teacher and pupil should begin their work together with this tacit understanding and the recognition of the right of either at any time to withdraw freely and with good will, from the relationship. I believe the teacher is "karmically" responsible for all he gives which the pupil accepts; and that the pupil, in his turn, must be deeply aware of how the teacher is voluntarily jeopardizing his own spiritual welfare in the dangerous task of striving to give guidance to another.

If these attitudes are accepted by both teacher and pupil, inevitably there occurs a profound sense of sharing a common spiritual destiny. Each gives the other a love and a trust which endure against all difficulties. Each knows, wherever he may be and whatever may befall, that the strength of the other is as his own. And each knows that in their inmost relationship neither is teacher or pupil, but both are brothers growing together in the greater life of God. They are to create a relationship which exemplifies what all human relationships should be.

This concept need be carried but a single step further. It is usually true that a teacher has more than one pupil. In many groups, where the work remains personality-centered, there is rivalry among students to be the favored one of the teacher, to have exclusive affection and attention, and presumably to win a dispensation of shortcomings and a short cut into the spiritual kingdom. Among advanced workers such selfishness is either a minor problem or nonexistent. The relationship is simply fraternal, each offering what is unique in himself to complement the others. The true teacher is one's own spiritual self; and the father of the group is, of course, God.

2. THE NATURE OF THE GURU

The guru occupies a unique and vital role in the spiritual development of Hindu and Tibetan Buddhist aspirants. Without a guru, these aspirants believe, enlightenment is impossible. The guru is regarded as one who, having obtained some degree of enlightenment himself, can impart it to others who are qualified. Enlightenment can be attained, in all but rare instances, only with the help of an enlightened one; and therefore the guru is deeply revered as "he upon whom one's salvation depends."

The true guru is one whose wisdom and love are unmistakably evident in his actions; whose insight is the product of intuitive experience rather than of book knowledge; who has mastered himself and surrendered himself totally to a Greater One; who, in tranquil detachment, is able to perceive the nature, the problems, and the needs of his pupil; who is selfless, asking nothing for himself from the pupil, and whose one concern is to aid the pupil into enlightenment; who is able to recognize instantly the few with psychic affinity who are destined to be his pupils; and who is capable of transmitting, with extraordinary inspiration, "his great light to light the pupil's little seed of light."

The guru is regarded as being one's spiritual father, and more important than one's father by blood. It is the guru, according to general belief, who gives spiritual birth; and, spiritually speaking, one is the guru's descendent and inheritor. One finds his own guru when the time is right, as inevitably as he became the son of his father by blood. When the pupil is ready, it has been said from ancient times, the Teacher appears.

One's spiritual lineage is of vital importance. For example, members of the Ka-Gyu-Pa sect in Tibet trace the transmittal of their teaching and the ultimate source of Divine Grace from the Buddha Dorje-Chang (Vajra-Dhara) to a line of celestial gurus, then to an apostolic guru in the world, and from him to subordinate gurus, one of whom may be one's own. In guru-yoga (practiced by many both in India and Tibet), which requires worshipful contemplation of one's guru in his enlightened aspect—never as a personality—the meditator is often advised to consider his own immediate teacher as a channel for, or a reflection of, the divine guru. This constitutes a recognition of the source of the spiritual gifts which are transmitted to one, and is by no means a device used by the immediate guru to enhance his own status.

Thus the true guru is more than merely a spiritual teacher. He is one's closest point of approach to a spiritual line which stretches from earth to heaven, from man to the Absolute. He is like an outlet for a distant power station. He transmits the stuff of enlightenment in one or both of two ways: he can initiate one in certain teaching and meditation techniques; or, when the pupil is prepared, he can transmit directly the divine grace, in effect making the student, on his own, another outlet of the celestial source. Even if the pupil himself becomes a guru, he subordinates himself to his own guru, whose spiritual descendent and inheritor he is.

The guru obviously has a mortal side which affects him with many very human problems. But one's essential relationship with the guru is through his infinite being, that eternal aspect which enables him to be a source of as much enlightenment as one is capable of absorbing. Hence, the tantric saying: "Never think of the guru as a mortal." A true guru will make you understand he is nothing in himself; it is that which he transmits which is all-important. The spirit of this attitude toward one's preceptor may be seen even in these few stanzas from the "Hymn to the Guru" (*Vishwa-sara-Tantra*):

> Salutations to the guru who has made it possible to realize Him by whom all this world, animate and inanimate, movable and immovable, is pervaded . . .
>
> Salutations to the guru who is the Supreme Spirit, eternal and serene . . .
>
> Salutations to the true guru who is the embodiment of the bliss of Brahman and the bestower of supreme happiness, who is himself detached, Knowledge personified, beyond duality, who is like the sky, who is indicated by such Vedic dicta as "Thou art That," and who is One, eternal, pure, immovable . . .

And hear Swami Vivekananda: "Religion, which is the highest knowledge and the highest wisdom, cannot be bought, nor can it be acquired from books. You may thrust your head into all the corners of the world, you may explore the

Himalayas, the Alps, and the Caucasus, you may sound the bottom of the sea and pry into every nook of Tibet and the desert of Gobi, you will not find it anywhere, until your heart is ready for receiving it and your teacher has come. And when that divinely appointed teacher comes, serve him with childlike confidence and simplicity, freely open your heart to his influence, and see in him God manifested. Those who come to seek truth with such a spirit of love and veneration, to them the Lord of Truth reveals the most wonderful things regarding Truth, Goodness, and Beauty." [2]

3. THE SPIRITUAL ADVISER AND THE PSYCHIATRIST

Sometimes we hear people say, "If I get mixed up inside I'll visit a psychiatrist, not a spiritual adviser." We will assume, of course, that those who make this remark distinguish between qualified psychiatric and spiritual counselors and the host of incompetents in both fields who cater to the ignorant. But the remark is regrettable because it shows a grave misunderstanding of the actual roles of the spiritual adviser and the psychiatrist. Certainly, for people whose problems are severely neurotic or psychotic, nothing could be more sensible than to consult a psychiatrist. The psychiatrist's job is to restore emotionally and mentally disturbed people to normalcy. The spiritual adviser's task is to assist normal people to achieve spiritual supernormalcy. The psychiatrist is a specialist among doctors; the spiritual adviser, a specialist among teachers. The approach of both is alike in that they

[2] Swami Vivekananda, *Bhakti-Yoga*. Ninth edition. Calcutta, Advaita Ashrama, 1955.

attempt fundamentally to help those who come to them to help themselves. But one has his eye on returning the individual to society; the other, on returning the individual to God.

4. "ALL THINGS ARE MY GURUS"

Since everything which exists is pervaded by the life of God, and since we can learn from everyone and everything in creation, we may call anyone or anything, in a special sense, our guru. "From Brahma to a blade of grass," the *Kaula Tantras* say, "all things are my gurus." But in a more precise usage, the guru is he who is our primary source of immediate and specific spiritual assistance; and still more particularly, he who is capable of awakening our inmost self. "The guru is only one," Sri Ramakrishna declares, "but upa-gurus [3] may be many. He is an upa-guru from whom anything whatsoever is learned." For the Indian or Tibetan aspirant, there can be no possibility of enlightenment until his own guru— whoever he may be, however extraordinary or ordinary he may seem to others—appears and says quietly, "At last— you are ready and you have come." Then, though all things are his gurus, all things become one; and the One is his own.

5. THE SPIRITUAL SIGNIFICANCE LATENT IN EVERY MOMENT

Indian spiritual teachers work continuously to teach their pupils to look for the spiritual significance latent in every

[3] upa-guru (pronounced "oo-pah goo-roo")—secondary teacher.

moment of life. Rarely do they miss an opportunity to make a point that may awaken new insight. And sometimes, when the pupil's moment of deeper understanding arrives, he senses suddenly that the teacher had carefully planned the occasion long before.

Once, for example, while I was walking along a steep mountainside path with a swami, we came to a place where the path simply disappeared. Where there had been a firm shelf of soil, now there was only a sharply slanting ledge of rough gray stone. I paused, looking at the drop of at least five hundred feet below the ledge. The swami chuckled. "Don't look down," he warned. "Look straight ahead. Now, do as I tell you." On his instructions I removed my sandals and buckled them to my belt. "Go slowly," he advised, "and remember—look only ahead." After the longest minute of my life, I reached the other side, and soon the swami was beside me. After a short search we found the path again. Then we sat down to rest. "Look only ahead," I mused aloud, putting on my sandals. All at once I smiled, struck with the fact that the swami's words were the answer to a problem I had been discussing with him earlier. The swami nodded, laughing quietly. "Yes, even when the way seems to be lost, look only ahead," he said. "The path will then be found again. Remember this, my son, in moments of difficulty." It wasn't until later, when I saw a broader and safer path far below us, that I realized the swami had deliberately chosen the more difficult path.

6. THE GURU'S LOVE

You may come to him for a few seconds, then go away and do whatever you will. His love is unchanging.

You may deny him to himself and to yourself, then curse him to any who will listen. His love is unchanging.

You may become the most despised of creatures, then return to him. His love is unchanging.

You may become the enemy of God Himself, then return to him. His love is unchanging.

Go where you will; do what you will; stay however long you will; and come back to him. His love is unchanging.

Abuse others; abuse yourself; abuse him; and come back to him. His love is unchanging.

He will never criticize you; he will never minimize you; he will never desert you. Because, to him, you are everything and he himself is nothing.

He will never deceive you; he will never ridicule you; he will never fail you. Because, to him, you are God-nature to be served and he is your servant.

No matter what befalls, no matter what you become, he awaits you always. He knows you. He serves you. He loves you.

His love for you, in the changing world, is unchanging.

His love, beloved, is unchanging.

7.   THE IMPATIENT CHELA

There was once a chela, earnest but impatient, who began to wonder if his guru were not deliberately withholding from him the key to truth. Determined to force a showdown, he tied up his few belongings in a cloth. Then, confronting his old guru, he said: "Sir, by now you must certainly know what my motive is, that more than anything in this transient world I yearn to know what eternal truth is. Then I beseech you, O enlightened one, to enlighten me: give me that knowledge which, when known, is the answer to every question. But," he added, despairingly, "if you will not, if you cannot, I must leave at once."

Then the guru, perceiving what was in his worried pupil's mind, instructed him quietly: "Go fetch all the scriptures you have been studying." The youth did so. "Now, go return them to the town pundit to whom they belong," the teacher said. "But, sir—" the chela began to protest; then, wonderingly, he gathered up the books and left. When the chela had returned the books and was with his old guru again, the teacher smiled strangely—"Now recite to me what you consider the basic truths in those books you have studied so long and so hard. And state why you think these particular truths are paramount." The chela, confident he could meet the request without difficulty, began to speak; and as he stated the truths he believed to be fundamental, and his reasons for supporting them, he warmed to his task and his words flowed. Striding back and forth, as if addressing a multitude, he declaimed the message of the books, and temporarily forgot his underlying doubt and despair. About an hour later, launching on his conclusion, he turned to his guru to try to see the impact of his eloquence.

But the old guru, in a sense, had just gone away. Radiant-faced, as a man could appear only in the presence of God, the guru sat serenely on the heights of samadhi. The abashed pupil suddenly sat down. At first he stared blankly—never before having seen his guru in samadhi. Slowly, as he gazed upon his teacher's face, and its great love and wisdom became apparent to him for the first time, he felt his impatience draining away and a new understanding, a new love, rushing in. After many minutes the chela forced himself to arise, to unpack his few possessions and restore them to their usual place. Then, again, he sat down before his old guru.

The period in samadhi lasted a long time. But the chela awaited his guru, patiently.

8. THE PUPIL'S QUALIFICATIONS

What distinguishes the advanced student of the spiritual life from the beginner? Or, to put the question another way, what are the qualifications for a chela who wishes to begin the most difficult, although the most rewarding, disciplines and studies of "the razor-edged path"?

There are four characteristics of the advanced pupil, according to Vedantic teachers. These characteristics, or qualifications, are known as the *sadhanachatushtaya*, or the four instruments of spiritual knowledge; and they may also be called the disciplines necessary to those who seek self-knowledge, or God-realization.

Sadananda,[4] in his *Vedantasara,* "the essence of Vedanta" (an introduction to the standard works of Vedanta), states the four requirements thus:

> The means to the attainment of knowledge are these: discrimination between the permanent and the transient; renunciation of the enjoyment of the fruits of action, in this world and hereafter; "the six treasures," such as control of the mind, and so forth; and the desire for liberation.

First, the pupil should have *viveka,* discrimination. He should be able, to an unusual degree, to separate the permanent from the impermanent, the real from the unreal. He should act in a manner reflecting his realization that his body, emotions, and mind, his desires, fears, and ambitions, belong to the phenomenal realm. He should perceive that beyond the changing is the unchanging, and that the Self within is identical with the Absolute, Brahman, which, Sadananda declares, "alone is the permanent Substance" and "all things other than it are transient." Because of this insight into where truth is to be found, the pupil is not deceived by mundane distractions.

Second, the pupil's life, both inner and outer, should exemplify *vairagya,* renunciation. He should know that all pleasures, because they are the products of action, are transient; that many worldly pleasures destroy character, compounding one's ignorance, impurity, and suffering; that many other pleasures, seemingly harmless in themselves, distract

[4] Sri Sadananda Yogindra Saraswat, who wrote his work probably sometime in the fifteenth century, was a famed scholar-illuminate and member of the monastic order founded by Shankaracharya.

the truth-seeker from his quest of the changeless. He should be nonattached to everything of a temporal nature. He should be detached even in his thought of whatever rewards may accrue to him in the life hereafter. He should renounce every distraction, however bedeviled with blandishments, which obstructs his exile's end in God.

Third, the pupil should have the *shatsampatti*, the six treasures. These are *shama*, calmness—the inner poise which comes with continuous contemplation of the Supreme Reality; *dama*, self-control—the restraint of the lower nature from every activity except the pursuit of the real; *uparati*, self-settledness—the mental ability to restrain the lower nature, temporarily governed by *shama* and *dama*, from again pursuing the unreal; *titiksha*, forbearance—the ability to endure, with detachment, everything arising from any of the pairs of opposites (such as heat and cold, or pain and pleasure); *samadhana*, perfect concentration—the steady centering of awareness on the nature of the Absolute as interpreted by the scriptures and one's guru; and *shraddha*, faith—the affirmative and intuitive attitude of heart and mind which enables the chela to respond to and to accept scriptural truth as his teacher expounds it.

And fourth, the pupil should have *mumukshutwam*, the yearning for spiritual liberation. When the foregoing three qualifications have been fulfilled, then the fourth may be achieved, and having it the pupil may be said to be truly ready to experience absolute knowledge. This is not a selfish craving, and is not to be confused with emotional fearfulness, frustration, or restlessness; this is the wise and loving consequence of a single-minded dedication of being to God.

It signifies the flowering of consciousness in the unification of subconscious "spiritual impulse," conscious spiritual motivation, and some effective degree of superconscious will. Every aspect of the lower nature is subject to this aligning and integrating compulsion; and the chela will no longer accept spiritual substitutes, whether emotional devotion, the performance of duty, or intellectual discussion and book knowledge. He now must have the unitive experience of God-nature. All else is subordinated to this yearning for realization; no internal or external obstacle can stand in his way for long; ignorance is his enemy; suffering, the casual parasite of his necessary condition; and sacrifice, whatever its nature, is a welcome gift to be proffered to Him who possesses and pervades even the least of sacrifices. For the chela who has it, *mumukshutwam* is the straight advancing line, without haste or hesitation, to the interior point of the God-nature.

Other qualifications for the consecrated student may be advanced; the world religions, and their various schools, have many to suggest. But however the advanced pupil may be defined, the indispensable qualification is the perpetual practice of *mumukshutwam*—to "love the Lord thy God with all thy heart, and with all thy soul, and with all thy mind, and with all thy strength . . . and . . . thy neighbor as thyself."

9. HOW TO TELL A CHELA

"You can tell the true chela from the wishful thinker and the pretender in a very simple way," an elderly Himalayan guru once told me. "The pretender wants praise and power; the wishful thinker wants the easy delusion of an unending dream state; but the true chela, who knows himself to be a terribly incomplete self, wants God, at any price at all."

12. SIGNPOSTS ON THE PATH

I. THE NEED TO BE READY

I once heard a Buddhist *bhikshu* [1] try to explain how use-less advanced spiritual instruction is until the pupil is ready to receive it. "Some years ago," he said, "the son of one of the wealthiest maharajas in India was married to the daugh-ter of an equally wealthy maharaja of a neighboring state. The young prince, who had never needed anything and who had always had everything, was especially taken with one present which, out of all, seemed to him to be perfection itself. The gift was *a silver tongue-scraper*. As useless as this is advanced spiritual teaching for one who is unprepared for it."

[1] *Bhikshu* (pronounced "beek-shoo")—title of a fully ordained Buddhist monk.

2. ON THE CHOICE OF COMPANIONS

At every stage of the spiritual life, but never so urgently as in the beginning, we need the companionship of the holy-minded. And we need to avoid the company of those who consciously or unconsciously contemn religious values. There is a simple reason for this. When we are in the presence of a genuinely spiritual person, we are deeply inspired by sensing our own God-nature more purely and more nobly manifested in him. This God-nature, the divine essence in each of us, is the fact on which we base the increasingly apparent brotherhood of all the truly spiritual, regardless of the faiths they profess. In these God-representatives, we see the embodiment of the truth we seek and the demonstration of our highest ideals; so that by being with them, by studying them, we learn subtleties beyond the grasp of words.

Similarly, when we are with those who resist or deny spiritual things, we are aware only of their elaborately defended egos. We feel rebuffed by their exaggerated individualism, their self-importance, their criticism. Their desires, their fears, their ambitions wrongly evoke our own; and, unless we are wary, we are driven to shut out their influence by erecting our own barriers of separateness and selfishness. Their insensitivity to the Spirit tends invariably to dull our own receptivity to higher truth.

In the initial stages of the spiritual life, before our own inner life is steadied, we are not selfish to shun those who are indifferent to our ideals, or who even despise them. This is a measure of self-protection and, for some aspirants, the difference between success and failure.

3. THE BULL AND THE KITTEN

A farmer had a pet bull of which he was very fond. But one day the farmer was given a kitten. Soon, to the dismay of the bull, the farmer began to lavish most of his attention on the playful little newcomer. At first the bull became sad, and the farmer seemed not to notice. Then the bull became sulky, but the farmer ignored him still. Later the bull became angry. One morning while the farmer and the kitten were out for a walk, the bull smashed headlong into a new haystack and laid it flat. The farmer did notice that; he gave the bull a very hard beating. For days after, while the farmer played happily with the kitten, the bull brooded on his sorrowful situation. Finally, while meditating in the farthest corner of the pasture, the bull reluctantly concluded the farmer no longer liked bulls. He liked kittens. Very well, he decided, he would study the wonderful behavior of this small creature! He then spied on the kitten for many days. Gradually it struck him that the kitten did two things which the farmer seemed especially to enjoy. So, one evening when the farmer had poured milk into a saucer and was just about to call the cat, the bull raced up and began to lap at the milk in the mincing way the kitten did. For a while the farmer laughed very loudly, now and then pouring extra milk. Then the bull, becoming clumsy, broke the saucer. That the farmer did not appreciate at all. He scolded the bull. But the bull, cheered greatly by the farmer's first laughter, did not despair. After all, his best trick was still to come. He remembered that above everything the farmer liked the kitten to sit in his lap. Patiently he waited until the farmer had finished his supper and then came to sit upon the front steps. The bull walked quietly up. Fortunately the farmer seemed to be dreaming of pleasant things. His eyes were closed. Ah, the bull thought happily, here goes!

The next day at dawn in the farmer's truck, bound for the nearest cattle market, go he did.

Moral: *Don't be a bull about being yourself.*

4. A BRIDGE OF PRAYERS

Tramping through a mountain valley near Sikkim, my guide and I came to a raging deep stream, and there was nothing to do except cross it on one of those nearer-my-God-to-Thee flimsy bamboo footbridges for which the Himalayas are notorious.

Halfway out, with the split-bamboo underfooting rocking crazily away to the left, and my swaying hand support stretching off to the right, I paused at what must have been a forty-five degree angle to ask my guide if he thought he was able to drag whatever was left of me out of the stream.

My guide, showing no concern at all, roared with laughter. "It is a good little bridge! It is a bridge of prayers!" he shouted. "But remember—he who crosses here must answer his own prayers!"

5. WORSHIP VERSUS ENTERTAINMENT

After the elaborate examples of showmanship we sometimes encounter nowadays under the guise of church services, I feel the way a friend did, who was leaving church after a service highlighted by six kinds of singing, string music, organ music, a pageant, peppy guest speakers, and a chart-illustrated account of the financial status of the church. Turning to his wife he declared wearily, "Now we can go home and pray."

6. MINDING ONE'S OWN BUSINESS

The science of minding your own business is to know what your business is. The art of minding your own business is to let others mind theirs. This is a sizeable problem when we begin to serve others. To serve as effectively as we would like to serve would call for the intellect of a da Vinci, the heart of a St. Francis, the finesse of a Franklin, the judgment of a Solomon, the wealth of a Croesus, the humor of a Cervantes, and the energy of a ten-year boy trying to escape a bath. But we can make service easier if we recognize that our legitimate business is not to relieve another person of his responsibilities, but to assist him—with his permission—in meeting them. If an aspirant to service cannot do this, and do it with science and art, he should attempt to develop it in some harmless way, say, by performing such a potentially valuable social service as lecturing ten-year-olds on the virtue of the bath.

7. TWO ASPECTS OF GROWTH AS PAIN

Pain is inherent in the process of spiritual growth. We build a personality form just as a crab builds a hard shell. But to grow we have to do what the crab does: shuck the old shell, go soft-shelled for an interlude of suffering, and live it out until the new shell is built. During this period between personality forms, we are low on defense, as the soft-shelled crab is. But the process of true growth is a constant building, outgrowing, discarding, and building new forms, until at last the personality is a purely receptive and permanently flexible instrument of the spiritual self. The form to be eliminated is always a set of values around which the personality has crystallized; and the new form to be created is always a more selfless, a more inclusive set of values. During this time, when our most cherished values are in flux, we need to be stubbornly faithful to the daily practice of our spiritual disciplines.

As we elevate and stabilize and strengthen our state of spiritual consciousness, we increasingly discover the eternal laws which regulate all life. And as we discover these, we become more and more acutely aware of the discrepancies between them and the behavior of mankind at large. Painfully we begin to be aware that humanity is less noble, as a whole, than we had ever imagined. As our spiritual insight deepens, the magnitude of wrong human values will appear to increase correspondingly. For example, we see—sometimes with profound shock and suffering—how vast is the gulf between the pure principle experienced in meditation and its abuse and neglect in normal everyday life. Yet, when some day we vividly experience the oneness of the God-nature in ourselves and in every unit of humanity, we know how inextricably involved in mankind each of us is; and this realization is one of the greatest incentives for service to others. But the preparation for a life of service is the tenacious devotion to perfecting the controllable little world of oneself. The external world may seem to be plunging absurdly and insanely to destruction; yet the realm of the self has to be transformed into a little God-world. And when that small world which one governs becomes ablaze with love and wisdom, others will be drawn to it and find there an unfailing source of compassionate warmth and inspiration.

8. CONFESSIONS OF THE CHELAS

A guru once requested his seven new chelas to bring before him a representation of what each considered his greatest barrier to God-realization.

"I could find God easily," the first declared, holding up a small bag of coins, "if it were not for my love of money."

"I could find God easily," the second stated, producing a list of grievances against his brother pupils, "if it were not for my love of criticizing."

"I could find God easily," the next raged, thrusting forth the photograph of a man, "if it were not for my love of hating my enemy."

"I could find God easily," the fourth sighed, showing several large packets of letters, "if it were not for my love of being liked."

"I could find God easily," the fifth confessed, placing the guru's extra robe around his own shoulders, "if it were not for my love of pretending to be what I am not."

"I could find God easily," the sixth said, pointing to a girl waiting at the edge of a distant wood, "if it were not for my love of women."

"I could find God easily," the last wept, prostrating himself humbly and empty-handed before the guru, "if it were not for my love of myself."

The teacher sat silently, studying his chelas. Then—"You will all find God easily," the guru said gently, "as soon as God is your only love."

9.   LINES FOR EGO

As with my upheld thumb
I cover the immensity of the sun,
so with my little ego, my Lord,
I veil Thy all-pervadingness.

10.   SOME REFLECTIONS ON SUFFERING

It is peace from ourselves we need most. Most of us are perpetually at war within ourselves. The incompatibility of our motives makes internal conflict inevitable. Until the subconscious, conscious, and superconscious areas of the mind are integrated into a God-filled whole, the interior warfare continues and there is no end to suffering. Desires and fears fight each other; these clash with entrenched attitudes and ambitions; the selfish aspects of being oppose the selfless; and then, when the personality has achieved relative stability, the ego begins its final and most bitter battle: its rebellion against

God-nature. Then we experience the most intense suffering of all.

Because most of us are devoted mainly to ourselves and our personal interests, we prefer to believe that our suffering is caused by others. We know that suffering generally appears when our relationships with others go wrong. But the chief role an opponent plays in our suffering is to dramatize and to focalize for us the raging, irresolvable conflict of our own personality forces. The source of suffering is always within us. There is a pattern to the appearance of suffering: conflict arises; it appears impossible to resolve it; we become frustrated; and we begin to suffer. The conflict may originate wholly within us, as in an opposition between instinctual desire and reasoning; or it may be triggered by the opposition of another individual, whose values are at odds with our own. But suffering will occur only if there is some division of our own moral forces; only if our opponent's words and actions succeed somehow in dividing us against ourselves; only if the healing power of intelligent love is lost and the ego selfishly asserts its rights over the rights of others.

Suffering has been called a creative factor. But it may also leave us comparatively unchanged, or it may have a viciously destructive effect upon us. Suffering has been called the functioning of justice; but in many cases it may also seem to be a malfunctioning of justice. Suffering has been called a law of spiritual growth; and this, it would seem, is nearer the truth. Because if life has no capacity for pain it would be destroyed by pleasure; if it had no capacity for pleasure it would be destroyed by pain. Death always awaits at the extremities of pain and pleasure. Thus pain, whether physical or emotional-mental, is a warning to us to gather our total life-resources to resist whatever it is which causes pain; yet, in mental suffering, we are rarely ever able to reason clearly, so that this truth has to be acted upon in advance, to prepare us for the certain onslaughts of suffering. And this warning means, to the spiritual worker, to work steadily and earnestly to eliminate the real cause of suffering, the ego, and to fill its place with God-nature.

But is it not true, some will say, that we may suffer because of our knowledge of the sufferings of others? Yes, we may suffer, if our knowledge results in conflict within us. The difference in reaction between an aspirant and a saint is that the first has an emotionally involved pity and the latter a spiritually detached compassion. One reaction stimulates emotion; the other, the spiritual self. Perhaps the most compassionate person present at the scene of an accident is the doctor; and usually he is also the most detached person there, and therefore the most capable. Excessive pity weakens us, draining our nervous energy through overstimulated emotion; but compassion strengthens us, mobilizing our spiritual energies, galvanizing our full resources of being for intelligent selfless action. Perfect love is entirely objective; it permits no emotional or mental distortion. In time of trouble, instead of wringing its hands in anguish, it uses those hands to go to work tenderly and wisely. The saint's compassion is radiated impartially to every living creature at all times, so that there is no inner change in his nature in the presence of a suffering person. He knows that pain, like pleasure, is an innate factor of life on this side of God-realization.

We must not believe it is a function of religion to deliver us from suffering; rather, its function is to enable us to pass safely through suffering. Religion can teach us that suffering is inevitable in spiritual growth. It can teach us that the source of suffering is the ego and its refusal to sacrifice its own interests to those of the divine self. It can teach us that suffering is normal until there is no longer separation from God. But what it can ultimately teach us best is how to let the ego die naturally to give place to God-nature. And the ego begins to disintegrate under the powerful impact of selfless love; self-renunciation ceases gradually to be an ideal and becomes a fact of being; and then, when there is no egoistic obstruction to God-nature, suffering has an end. The end is in the peace from ego-born conflict, and in the greater peace of eternal refuge in God.

13. THE GOD WE LOVE

1. HEAVENLY WHO'S WHO

The gods, goddesses, godlings, angels, spirits, devas, dakinis, and other supernatural entities acknowledged by the worshipful members of humanity are literally countless. Hinduism alone is said to account for about 330,000,000; Buddhism and Shinto add many more millions; and if we begin to reckon with the entities honored by primitive tribesmen, we may arbitrarily cease to add to our *Heavenly Who's Who* at the figure of a billion.

This is a fact which many people, especially Christians, Jews, and Muslims, find exceedingly distressing. How many people must be praying to nonexistent deities!

The snowlit summit of Kanchenjunga can be viewed from numerous angles and distances. If the range is viewed only from a valley nearby, one may never behold more than one of the lower peaks of the great mountain. I have seen it through mists as the merest suggestion of a crest, or concealed to various degrees by cloud and rain; and I have seen it darkly outlined and faintly glowing at night, a luminous golden in the early morning, dazzling white at midday, or touched differently with shades shifting from pink to purple at every sunset. However I strive to describe it, however I labor to capture it in words, whatever insights it arouses, and whatever name I choose to give it, the mountain remains itself, unchanged by my regard, independent of my little knowledge and my puny judgment.

So with Godhead, Supreme Reality. However, unlike the mountain, God responds to us; every religion has its own evidence of some such response. How else could the major religions have endured for so long? The sincere orthodox exponent of one religion weeps for the sincerely orthodox of every other religion; yet is it not possible that the God we love, in His love, has other flocks of which the orthodox are unaware? And against the scalelessness of eternity is not man, in his few thousand years of religious history, an infant angrily opposing his own demands against the wise will of a loving parent? When the infant cries out, the parent does not demand to be addressed by any single preferred name.

Behind the names we give the Godhead, the celestial parts into which we attempt to divide its oneness, it remains itself, answering to every sincerely given name, answering when called upon by the names of its imagined parts or attributes, and even answering to names which must be wrong but which, conceived in honest ignorance, are the only names one may know. The true worshipper, whatever his faith, knows he is not praying to a name alone; his prayer is to the Godhead beyond the name, the reality whose ultimate name no man knows. Perhaps there is no ultimate name. Lao Tzu, long ago, declared: "The name which can be named is not the name." The ancient Hindu sighed: "I pray to the One without a name." Meister Eckhart addressed his prayer to "the Nameless Nothing." Perhaps, then, there is no ultimate name. Whether we say Godhead, Brahman, Tao, Allah, or Absolute Reality; or the One Life, the Primal Cause, the All-Pervading Energy, the Law, or the Presence; or Truth, Will, Love, Intelligence, or Beauty; or Father, Mother, Son, Spirit, or Friend, we mean the same. A name is useful only to distinguish one entity from another; therefore what need is there for a name for the One which contains and sustains all that which is, apart from which there is no other?

The name we choose immediately is the Christ, that name being the way through which we approach the Godhead. Similarly the Hindu may say Vishnu, Shiva, or Shakti, before he addresses Brahman. The Jew may say Messiah before he contemplates Jehovah. The Buddhist may say Sakyamuni before he reaches toward Absolute Reality. The Sufi Muslim may say Beloved before he meditates on Allah. The personal God, the deity who lives among men or the deity who seems closer because humanly understandable aspects are attributed to him, is the gateway; he is the friend who introduces the worshipper to the inmost kingdom; he is the known who accompanies the disciple towards the unknown, towards God-without-attribute, towards namelessness in God-without-name.

2. RABI'A'S LOVE OF GOD

Sometimes, when we wonder about how much we love God, we might do well to remember Rabi'a, the eighth-century Sufi woman saint. Rabi'a trusted completely in God to provide her with the few necessities her life seemed to require. Refusing her friends' urgings to accept financial help, she explained: "I should be ashamed to ask for worldly things from Him to whom the world belongs; how, then, can I ask anything from those to whom nothing really belongs?" When the Governor of Basra (Iraq), Mohammed Sulayman, offered her a rich dowry to become his wife, she refused: "You should not distract me from God for a single moment. My Lord can give me all you offer, even double it." Rabi'a believed wholly in the surrender of her personal will to God's will. "If I will a thing," she said humbly, "and my God does not will it, I shall be guilty of unbelief." Once, because she rarely mentioned Paradise, Rabi'a was asked, "But don't you desire Paradise?" And she replied softly: "It is the Lord of the House I need: what have I to do with the House?" "Do you love God?" Rabi'a was asked one day. "Yes," she answered instantly and happily. "Then do you hate Satan?" the question came. "No," she retorted at once, "because my love of God leaves no room for hating Satan. My love of God has so possessed me that no place remains for loving or hating anyone, only for loving Him." And this was Rabi'a's prayer: "O my Lord, if I worship Thee for fear of hell, burn me in hell; if I worship Thee for hope of Paradise, exclude me from Paradise; but if I worship Thee for Thy own sake, withhold not from me Thy eternal beauty."

3. FROM ANIMISM TO MONOTHEISM

Without straying beyond the town limits of Kalimpong, we can study most of the stages in the evolution of religious consciousness.

There is *animism*—the belief that natural objects and aspects of nature are endowed with souls. Bonism, the religion of Tibet before Buddhism was introduced in the sixth century A.D., was characterized by belief in the existence of numerous good and evil spirits, spirits of heaven, of mountains and mountain passes, rivers and streams, trees, of certain localities, and of various other aspects and objects of nature. Tibetans, including our Kalimpong neighbors, still believe in such spirits and make ritual offerings to them. The belief is not restricted to Tibetan Buddhists, but is an accepted part of orthodox Buddhism everywhere, authority for the belief being contained in early and basic Buddhist texts. As for Hinduism, in its Vedic stage the principal gods were Indra (rain), Agni (fire), and Surya (sun); and orthodox Hinduism, like Buddhism, contains a living stratum of animistic belief. To give two examples from farther away: in the West Indies and along the northern coast of South America, where every year violent storms howl up out of the ocean, the Carib Indians fearfully worshipped *Hurukan*, and the early Greeks, half a world away, trembled with awe before the destructive power of the evil monster of high wind and volcano, *Typhon*.

There is *animatism*—the belief in an impersonal supernatural energy (akin in some ways to Bergson's *élan vital*), which may be a benevolent force or not. Polynesians call this energy *mana;* the Algonquin tribe of American Indians call it *manito. Mana* is regarded as the power which makes possible magic and miracles, and it is believed one will have such power if *mana* is strong in him.

There is *totemism*—the belief common, for example, among certain Indian tribes of the northwest coast of North America that the family or the tribe has a "blood" relationship with certain species of animal or plant life, which are given special veneration.

There is *fetishism*—the reverence and often worship of objects as various in nature as pebbles, claws, human bones, and meteorites believed to be endowed with magical properties. The use of protective charms is practiced the world over, charms such as the amulets worn by many Hindus and Buddhists in Kalimpong and the religious medals carried by some Christians.

There is *image worship*—the image being regarded as the dwelling place of a supernatural spirit or deity, or as embodying something of the power of the spirit or deity, somewhat in the way an electric current "indwells" a light bulb, or as a symbol intended only to aid worship of a spirit or deity.

There is *spiritism*—the belief that man is surrounded by and even influenced by good and evil spirits, not primarily or exclusively related to objects and aspects of nature, but independent entities in their own right. Originally the use of "holy water," in some religions, derived from the belief that it helped to banish evil spirits.

There is *ancestor worship*—the worship, common in India, China, and Japan, of the spirits of one's departed forebears. We see much of fetishism, image worship, spiritism, and ancestor worship in our mountain town.

There is *worship of divine descendents*—the worship of those believed to be descended from gods. In Shinto, every Japanese emperor is revered as a direct descendent of Amaterasu, goddess of the sun.

There is *guru-worship*—the worship of one's spiritual guide, whom Hindus call divine and Buddhists enlightened, the guru being regarded as an instrument or channel for a Celestial Guru.

There is *worship of divine agents*—the worship of those variously termed Agents of God, Masters, Bodhisattvas, Ministering Spirits, Guardian Angels, Great Rishis, True Saints, Elder Brothers, and Guides of the Race. Divine-Agent worship, though more esoterically practiced in Hinduism, is well-developed in Mahayana Buddhism as worship of the Bodhisattvas.

To adopt more inclusive terms, there is *polytheism*—the belief in many gods, but with no single god predominant; and *henotheism*—the belief in many gods, with one god acknowledged greatest. In polytheistic systems many of the gods personify forces of nature or virtue-ideals. Just as polytheism is a development of animism, so henotheism projects from polytheism, as it did in ancient Greece when Zeus was worshipped as the primary god of the Olympian pantheon, and as Jupiter of the Roman hierarchy.

Finally there is *monism*—the belief that underlying everything there is but one kind of substance or Ultimate Reality.

And *monotheism*—the belief in one God. The Supreme may be interpreted from a variety of intellectual viewpoints, but essentially as God Transcendent, separate from man and nature, or God Immanent, the divine essence of every entity of humankind and/or nature, or both. *Pantheism* is the belief that everything which exists, taken as a whole, is God; and *panentheism* is the belief that God is transcendent and immanent, that the Absolute both pervades everything which is and yet remains apart from it. From the austere viewpoint of Advaita Vedanta, Hinduism is a form of monotheism since, rather than denying many gods for one God, it contends that all the gods are united and identical in all-inclusive Brahman. Christianity, Judaism, and Islam are monotheistic religions, of course; and Christianity and Islam, at least, have established their landmarks on the Kalimpong scene.

So, in the little world of Kalimpong, we can look at the diverse guises of man's yearning to interpret his significance under the stars. We can see how he begins first with nature, then turns finally to himself. And how, in nature and himself, he discovers the Life of which he is a part.

4. FORBIDDEN SIKKIM AND THE MOUNTAIN GOD

I stood in the Royal Temple of Gangtok, the capital of forbidden Sikkim, and a priest of the temple reverently placed Kanchenjunga in my hands.

What I held, horrible and ancient but as beloved (the priest's eyes told me) as any object in this world can be—was the carved wooden face-mask of the spirit of Mount Kanchenjunga, used in the priests' annual ritual dance to the Spirit, in loving gratitude for his endless bounties.

"His mask, the other masks are some like it too," the young priest explained in halting English. "It is frightening to watch —so large, the face like blood, the sharp teeth, on top of the head the skull. It is this way, the way as in Tibet. The good ones have many bodies like the water has many pots. This way they seem so bad, it is to frighten the bad ones away."

Kanchenjunga: to the aboriginal natives of Sikkim, the Lepchas, *Konglo Chu,* the "Highest Veil of the Ice," from whose glacial snows the first man and woman were created; on whose wild fields the "Snowman," the Yeti, is said to roam; on whose far side is said to lie the Kingdom of Death. *Kanchenjunga:* to the Tibetans, who conquered Sikkim through the Buddhist saint Lhatsun Chempo and his handful of followers, "The Five Treasures of the Eternal Snow," home of a god who stores gold, silver, precious stones, corn, and sacred books, each to a peak.

Home of a god—*Kanchenjunga!* And this was the god, the Sikkimese say, who helped the Buddhist saint Lhatsun Chempo to find the best route into Sikkim. Ever since, the Buddhist priests have once a year donned masks, one of them the dominating mask of Kanchenjunga, and danced to thank him for his help.

And the sacred mask of Kanchenjunga I held in my hands, marveling at the benevolent wrath of the face, the wrath of a father who at Halloween makes the most ferocious-looking face he can and, to please his children, gently attempts to frighten them a little.

Now the priest, in his plum-red robe, was showing us other masks: a bone-white skull with a crown of five skulls; a parrot-lizardlike face with a pair of deadly long horns; a demon-seeming deity out of whose head grew a smaller replica of his own horror, and out of the second, like a smaller echo, another.

Earlier, after nearly two weeks of seeking a permit to enter this little Himalayan kingdom long closed to Westerners, my Western friend and I had quietly explored as much of Sikkim as the stringent laws permitted. We had come finally to this temple on a mountain facing the main trade passes into Tibet, and had the blessed fortune to meet a priest as curious about the West as we were about this part of the East. And he had shown us around the room used by the Dalai Lama on his occasional visits, with its shrine, religious objects, and *thang-kas*.[1] We had examined block-printed old Tibetan scriptures, wrapped in the prescribed coverings of yellow silk; we stood beside the huge gong of the temple, which the priest sounded lightly; and we held a fourteen-foot long Tibetan lamas' horn which, with an unexpected grin, the priest suggested I attempt to blow, and I did.

Now, proudly and movingly, surveying all the dance masks, the priest was asking my friend, "Like this in your country, you have anything?"

And my friend was shaking his head. "No—" he said, with understanding, "outside of the same truth you seek, no, not anything."

The face of the young priest suddenly brightened. "Truth," he said simply. "But that is *everything*."

---

[1] *Thang-ka* (pronounced "tong-kah")—a vividly colored religious painting, on cloth, framed by a broad border of silk brocade. The *thang-ka*, which may portray one of the Mahayana Buddhas or Bodhisattvas or a group of them or a deity and consort, is an object of contemplation in elementary forms of tantric meditation. While the size of the *thang-ka* may vary—I have seen some not much larger than the palm of my hand, and others which covered the wall of a monastery—all elements of the picture, such as proportions and colors, must conform to an ancient formula.

Bowing, I returned the mask of Kanchenjunga to the priest's hands.

5. HOW TO LOVE GOD

The first commandment of the spiritual life is to love God. But why should we love God? And how should we love God?

The simplest reason for loving God is that we are incomplete and unfulfilled until we consciously know ourselves as living and moving and having our being in God. Self-realization means God-realization. The very essence of love is that, when perfectly experienced, it is a relationship which obliterates itself in the total identification and oneness of the lover and the Beloved. And a basic law of the spiritual life is that through love of God which fuses with knowledge of Him we may achieve that unitive state which can be only faintly hinted at in such statements as "I live, yet not I, but God lives me." God lives in me as I live in a cell of my body. And in the perfected relationship made possible by love-wisdom, I may know myself as an individualized area of being in the life of God, until, in the disappearance of relationship, only God-nature, the Supreme Reality, aware of itself remains.

So the first manifestation of God we must learn to love rightly is our divine essence, the God-nature within us. The origin and center of being of each of us is in God, the "One God and Father of all, who is above all, and through all, and in you all" (Ephesians 4:6). By recognizing this innate divinity we can see that the second commandment, to love one's neighbor as oneself, is a variation of the first commandment; but where the first emphasizes God Transcendent, the second stresses God Immanent. Love the God-nature within your neighbor as the God-nature within yourself. Literally love your neighbor as yourself because, in your common God-nature, you and your neighbor are one. "The Ground of God and the Ground of the Soul are one and the same," Eckhart declares. "This self is Brahman," Yajnavalkya asserts. "One Reality, all-comprehensive, contains within itself all realities," Yung-chia Ta-shih says. "Behold but One in all things; it is the second that leads you astray," Kabir warns.

Our right love of the God-nature within subordinates all else to it. Only in this way may we be completed in the wholeness of God. Whatever tends to separate us from the unitive experience of Godhead has to be eliminated; and all that we are, all that we feel and think and do, must be dedicated to the glory of God. This involves a continuous practice of the presence of God; as with the saint, who means it profoundly when he says, I make my wrong desire subservient to right desire and all desires subservient to Thy will. I control my emotions so that Thy perfect love may be more purely reflected in my life. All my thoughts I turn to Thee, because of my love of Thee. Our right love of our neighbor is to serve the God-nature within him. The greatest service is always based on this recognition. Intelligent love, with the ultimate end of aiding others to realize their inherent divinity, becomes the criterion in our relationships with others. We express our love of God by always attempting to appeal to and to associate with the God-self in others. This involves a continuous practice of the presence of God in others; as with the saint who declares, I serve God by serving all His creation. I see God in all loving thoughts and deeds. I love God in everyone and everything, for He dwells indivisibly within all.

The next stage at which we may love and worship God is, in most religions, the least clearly defined. At this level we may love God as God is said to manifest Himself through His divine agents—variously called Messengers and Ministering Angels of God, the True Saints, the Masters of the Wisdom, the Inner Guides of Humanity, the Elder Brothers of the Race, and the Bodhisattvas; and, as a group, often referred to as the Spiritual Hierarchy, the Hierarchy of Saints or of Angels and Archangels, the Great Ashram, the Masters of the Kingdom, and the Government of Heaven. In many religions, God is believed to express His will not only through human workers but also through those great ones who, having achieved perfectibility from the human viewpoint, now comprise the leadership of the spiritual kingdom. It is contended that God, through these divine agents, may give guidance and aid to certain of His advanced human disciples. There are numerous stories in the major religions of specific individuals having been helped by such divine intervention; for example, Peter's escape from prison through the agency of an angel (Acts 12:11). To Protestant Christians these spiritual guides are real enough although little considered or worshipped; Catholics, on the other hand, pray to and through the saints in Heaven, and the Blessed Virgin Mary. The theological position of Judaism and Islam is roughly comparable to that of Protestant Christianity. The great majority of Hindus and Buddhists believe that direct divine guidance is a common experience among the most evolved disciples; that, in fact, the divine agent—the Celestial Guru—has an ashramic group of human disciples under his subjective protection and direction. Mahayana Buddhists have a fully developed doctrine and form of worship of the Bodhisattvas; and they believe that every exceptional disciple is brought within the guardianship of his destined master or Bodhisattva. It is also believed by many that frequently human beings are given guidance which they may be either slightly aware of or not aware of at all; and that only small numbers of servers are strongly conscious of and understand the source and purpose of their spiritual guidance, said to be given as suggestion and never as order. For most people, God always "works in mysterious ways His wonders to perform"; but to a few, when truly perceptive of God's will through them, the ways are less mysterious and even more awesome.

We may love God, next, as a personal God, as a Divine Person, as God-with-form, and especially as God is believed to have dwelled on earth among us. In the personal God is embodied the practical demonstration for humanity of God manifest; in the personal God is exemplified the perfection of the divinity innate within every human being; in the personal God is the way to Godhead, the truth of existence, and the life-in-God eternally. For the Christian He is the radiant, wise, and compassionately loving One we call the Christ, the Son of God, One with God the Father and the Holy Spirit. For the Hindu there are many personal Gods, with worship of them centered chiefly in the Ganapatya cult, the Vaishnava cult, the Shaiva cult, and the Shakta cult. In Mahayana Buddhism, with its multifaceted approach to the fulfillment of spiritual consciousness, the historic Buddha is regarded, if not as a personal God in the Christian or Hindu sense, as fulfilling the devotee's need for an exemplar, teacher, Enlightened One, being the object of devout worship. Although neither Judaism nor Islam acknowledges a God-with-form who has lived and moved among human beings, the great mystics of both have regarded the One God as having, in an aspect of His being, the approachability of a personal God. In Judaism He is addressed by and talks to His prophets; and in Islam, among the Sufis in particular, He is One who may be worshipped as the Beloved. And a similar level of worship of God-with-attribute, but not incarnated in human form, exists in Christianity with God the Father and the Holy Spirit; in Hinduism, with such deities as Brahma; while in Mahayana Buddhism—which maintains a conception of supernatural entities which Mahayanists refuse to describe, in approximation of Hindu or Christian conceptions, as God-with-attribute— there are such worshipped deities, or Buddhas-with-attribute, as Vairochana, Akshobhya, Ratna-Sambhava, Amogha-Siddhi, and Amitabha.

God-without-attribute—the Godhead of the Christian mystic and Nirguna Brahman, Parabrahman, the Supreme Reality, of the Hindu saint—is the ultimate journey's end of worshipful consciousness, in which even worship itself at last becomes impossible. It was of this final level of divinity, insofar as human consciousness appears capable of registering it, that St. Bernard, replying to the unaskable question, Who is God?, said in thoughtful and unavoidable evasion, "I can think of no better answer than, He who is." Eckhart, perhaps the most expressive of all the Christian saints of this highest God-realization, declares with saintly desperation: "Meanwhile, I beseech you by the eternal and imperishable truth, and by my soul, consider; grasp the unheard-of. God and

Godhead are as distinct as heaven and earth. Heaven stands a thousand miles above the earth, and even so the Godhead is above God. God becomes and disbecomes. Whoever understands this preaching, I wish him well. But even if nobody had been here, I must still have preached this to the poor box." At this peak of consciousness Ruysbroeck asserts, "We can speak no more of Father, Son, and Holy Spirit, nor of any creature, but only One Being, which is the very substance of the Divine Persons. There were we all one before our creation, for this is our superessence. There the Godhead is in simple essence without activity." Here is the God-Supreme out of which God manifest appears, appears in the world yet apart from it, immanent in every entity yet above all. Here is the Absolute which can be placed in no category, for Godhead is unique and contains within itself all categories. Here is the Ultimate One without second which transcends all attributes, for every attribute is a limitation, implying an opposite, and Godhead is without limitation and yet contains everything which is. Here is the indeterminate Absolute which no entity can enter into relationship with, for within itself are all entities and all apparent relationships. Here, as St. Catherine of Genoa impossibly says, uniting the two points of the Hindu saint's "That are thou": "My Me is God, nor do I recognize any other Me except God Himself." So there is one easiest trysting place where the wise in love may find Him: "Search in thy heart," Kabir cries, "search in thy heart of hearts; *there* is His place and abode." And Guru Nanak implores his disciples to remember: "The Precious Jewel, for which men go on pilgrimage, dwells within the heart. Pundits read and argue, but know not that which is within themselves." And as the poet of the *Parapuja* asks, grasping the unattainable paradoxical realization, "What place is there in which to invoke the infinite, or what can serve as a seat for Him who contains within Himself all existence?"

Sri Ramakrishna, true God-man of India and Earth, once told his followers about a salt-doll who, being curious to know the nature of the ocean, ventured down to the rim of the water and advanced confidently out into the sea . . .

Love is the harmony of His parts.

6. THE GARDENER'S GOD

When we lived in Shantiniketan, West Bengal, home of the university founded by Rabindranath Tagore, our gardener, a devout Hindu, followed our Christmas preparations with touching sympathy. When I explained our wish for a small evergreen tree his sympathy became magical assistance. Staring across the plains of rice fields, with their occasional islands of huts, coconut palms, and banana plants, I had despaired of ever finding an evergreen; but the gardener had not. He appeared one morning, to call at my window shortly after sunrise, staggering under a giant branch of a pine tree. And when I rushed outside to exclaim happily over it, he produced a small roll of wire, and we were soon creating together one of the loveliest Christmas trees I have ever seen. When I gazed toward the paddies and inquired where he had found the pine branch, the gardener's smattering of English was suddenly exhausted, but not his broad canary-swallowing grin. A few weeks later I felt I had a clue when, strolling through the university grounds, I discovered a little botanical garden.

On Christmas Eve several European friends joined us to behold the miracle of the tree, resplendently glittering with ornaments we had fashioned from tin cans, tinfoil, colored paper, and chains of scarlet berries. While we were talking I heard a light tapping at the door. It was the gardener. He was dressed in his best white shirt and *dhoti*. Clutched with both hands was a clay pot brimming with a great bunch of carefully arranged marigolds, which Hindus consider an auspicious flower. I opened the door for him. He crossed the room quickly, his eyes intent on the tree. Then, as he would have done before an image in his temple, he kneeled humbly, placing the marigolds as an offering before the Christmas tree, and bowed low and long and reverently. Suddenly, in that simple and generous expression of his love for God, a new dimension of Christmas came glowingly alive in that little room and in our hearts.

14. THE POWER IS LOVE

I. THE EAR-WHISPERED DOCTRINE

In the name of the God of Love whom I adore, and in the light of the personal integrity which makes that love for Him possible, I find it a hopeless enterprise to attempt to confine our God within the strait-jacket dogma of any single sect, or denomination, or even religion. He is, my incorrigible heart ceaselessly assures me, the One God of all humanity, of all His creatures and creations. If I dare to say it seems to me that one religious group is right, I become painfully aware of suggesting all other groups are wrong, or that they are less right than the group I might choose.

I am aware of the reasonable objections to such a stand. I am persuaded that every serious aspirant to truth or God-knowledge must work his way up through one of the major religious traditions. Every devotee needs a spiritual framework within which to begin to find himself; he needs a terminology and a symbolism. He needs a great body of religious experience against which his own experience may be tested and evaluated. He requires, even desperately, a method of work, a systematic set of disciplines. And he must have, out of the most complete sense of spiritual desperation, a God who is personal, who is his teacher and protector and guide and even saviour, and who is never any further away than the pounding of the universal surf of the One Life which breaks into the inmost quiet pools of his own heart.

For me this tradition is Christianity. He who helps my little understanding is the Christ. It is He who has attended the moments of my self-discovery. It is His saints who have given me a language, a map of the godly kingdom within to ponder and to follow, and a vivid account of the dangerous beauty of the way to His presence. He it is who has lodged Himself within a secret chamber of my heart, and whose home is there, this moment and forever, although His mansions are many—although, wherever anything of Godhead's is, He is there, everywhere.

Yet, it is impossible not to think that this or that group is closer or further from God-Truth. Perhaps my own environment has schooled me in spiritual illiteracy. But, for one who has known the Christ, all experience without Him seems to lie in an underworld of tangled darkness and ignorance. Still, I have seen and known and been warmly inspired by the God-nature in a living saint of Hinduism, and in another of Buddhism; I spoke with these two, and spoke more deeply in the wordless communication the heart alone can comprehend —wondering how it could be that God, without my Christ, could have made His home within these two, brothers of my soul. I spoke of Christ to one, who talked of Vishnu to me; and I exclaimed of the Son of God to the other, who murmured of Avalokitesvara endearingly. Then, because continuous interior experiment is vital for those who long to know divine truth more fully, I sought the deities of my friends. In one series of meditations, under my friend's instruction, I invoked Vishnu; in another series, again with guidance, I invoked Avalokitesvara; and I practiced these meditations diligently over many months. The meditations, to my mind, were successful; and yet, on every occasion that something happened, it invariably was this: my invocation of Vishnu or Avalokitesvara was answered by the inner presence of Him whom I have learned to know and love as the Christ. Others, admittedly, may repeat this experiment with totally different results. While I still believe that the teachings of one religious group may seem further away from truth than those of another group, I am now willing to admit that individuals within other groups may know God as intimately as any man finds possible.

Thus I spend most of my reading hours, and hours with preceptors of other religions, searching for a larger tradition than the one in which I have been trained, a tradition of truth great enough to include the saints of every religion. And this tradition—its names range from Leibniz's phrase *philosophia perennis* to the Ageless Wisdom—is, it seems to me, the living essence of every religion, and also represents the means of their transcendental unity in God. Every religion, like man himself, consists of body, soul, and spirit. Orthodoxy, what the masses of worshippers see and hear and do, is the body; liberalism, what some devotees discover as the life behind the forms and the symbols, is the soul; and universalism, what a few detect as the unchanging Supreme Reality sought by all religions, is the spirit.

Every major religion functions at these three general levels —which, to be sure, can be only arbitrarily separated. Jesus says repeatedly, "He that hath ears to hear, let him hear." A *Upanishad* text declares: "It is difficult for many even to hear about it [Brahman]; hearing about it, many do not comprehend. He is a marvel who can teach it, and he is able who finds it; and he is a marvel who knows it, taught by an able teacher." The second level may be characterized as the stage at which one has an intuitive grasp of the inner meaning of the publicly available teaching; and this level also includes much of the verbal instruction, uncommitted to writing.

Then let us turn briefly to the tradition of verbal teaching which, so far as the dwellers on the first level of understanding are concerned, is nonexistent.

But surely, I hear far voices faintly protest, such a tradition has never existed in Christianity! Has it, or has it not? There is, St. Basil writes, for those whose hearing is deeper than their ears, "a tacit and mystical tradition maintained down to our own times, and a secret instruction that our fathers observed without discussion and which we follow by dwelling in the simplicity of their silence. For they understood how necessary was silence in order to maintain the respect and veneration due to our Holy Mysteries. And in fact it was not expedient to make known in writing a doctrine containing

things that catechumens are not permitted to contemplate."
Hear St. Denys the Aeropagite, too: "The things that are be-
stowed uniformly and all at once, so to speak, on the Blessed
Essences dwelling in heaven, are transmitted to us as it were
in fragments and through the multiplicity of the varied symbols of the divine oracles. For it is on these divine oracles that
our hierarchy is founded. And by these words we mean not
only what our inspired masters have left us in the Holy
Epistles and in their theological works, but also what they have
transmitted to their disciples by a kind of spiritual and almost
heavenly teaching, initiating them from person to person in
a bodily way no doubt, since they spoke, but, I venture to
say, in an immaterial way also, since they did not write. But
since these truths had to be translated into the usages of the
Church, the apostles expressed them under the veil of symbols
and not in their sublime nakedness, for not everyone is holy,
and, as the Scriptures say, knowledge is not for all." That is,
the discipline of the secret, is ready only for those who know
what they ask, who are prepared to receive what they seek,
and who are willing to become that which is opened within
them. Yes, the fading whispers argue, but you speak of a
dead and unreal tradition. Or do I speak of a tradition which,
for those of the first level of understanding, has never existed
and perhaps never will?

Unique to Christianity? Ask the persecuted Sufi, who has
protected with his life what he knows, what he received,
what in becoming he is. Ask the master yogis and the rishis of
Hinduism, who pass their wisdom and their power with infinite discrimination to the one, two, or three capable of selfless acceptance, and who speak of things no book on earth

ever contained or would be capable of depicting, for the fab-
ric of truth is not a web of reason but the luminous garment
of wholeness of being—the Word of God, one might suggest,
made flesh. Ask the rinpoches, the High Lamas of Tibet,
who pass on to their few "The Ear-Whispered Doctrine,"
the teaching too cruelly beautiful and awesome and understandable for most men to be able to bear—a teaching transmitted at the higher stages to those who, in the main, despair
of ever finding another ear ready to receive it. It is unique
only to one group, to those who know that the final authority
rests in no religious dogma, but in that which the little dogma
seeks to reflect.

Perhaps the almost unbridgeable chasm between the second and third levels is hinted at by St. Thomas Aquinas as
well as by anyone else. This scholarly man of God, who had
fought his way to the gate of heaven through unremitting
intellectual effort, had a vision several weeks before his death.
In St. Nicholas Church in Naples on St. Nicholas's Day the
good doctor, while celebrating the mass, beheld what he had
long sought. For days thereafter he lapsed into silence, aban-
doning the composition of his masterpiece, the *Summa*. Then,
not long before his leave-taking of earth, in reply to the question of why he no longer worked on what he had regarded
as a summary of spiritual truth, he confessed: "Because what
I have seen makes all that I have written mere chaff . . ."

There are, then, three levels of understanding: of human
nature, insisting on the infallibility of a single dogma; of the
soul, discovering a unity among the diverse groups which
comprise every religion; and of spirit- or God-nature, aware
of a Divine Plan wise and loving enough to embrace every

unit of humanity. The first is shouted in the market place, the second is discussed in the temple, and the third is whispered by God in the heart to Himself.

2. WHAT IS "SPIRITUAL"?

"Spiritual" is one of those words we are forced to use in order to distinguish between life in God and life in the material. Its connotations are liable to be wrong, however. Everything which exists has spiritual significance. Every desire of ours, every feeling, fear, anxiety, whim, emotion, dream, idea, ambition, and action has unbounded meaning. Every moment of life contains, if only we might read its import with sufficient insight, all that is necessary to reveal to us the nature of reality. Every experience we have ever had has brimmed over with spiritual implication, although we are trained not to recognize the continuous possibility of God-revelation. Below the superconscious level we are not nonspiritual, but potentially spiritual. As we grow through self-purification and renunciation, the lower nature begins to assume the quality of the spiritual self, then everything in existence begins to speak to us of God. We see how the One Life is all-pervasive. We understand why, when someone pounded on the door of Bayazid of Bistun, the Sufi saint, and called, "Is Bayazid there?" the old man cried out, "Is anybody here except God?" Because we begin to recognize, as one of the Eastern mystics wrote, that "God sleeps in the mineral, dreams in the plant, wakes to consciousness in the animal, to self-consciousness in man, and will awake to divine consciousness in the man made perfect." And because we be-

gin to understand why, when Rama told Vashistha he wished
to renounce the world in order to find God, the sage replied,
"But can you tell me where God is not? Is He apart from the
world that you wish to renounce it?" And because we begin
to comprehend St. Augustine's profound little prayer: "O
Lord, help me to perceive Thee. Help me to perceive myself,
for by knowing Thee I can know myself."

3. GOD-NATURE, LIKE A MOUNTAIN

The God-nature within is complete in itself; it is infinite,
illimitable, inexhaustible, eternally unchanging. Like a great
snow-crested mountain, God is always there. When we try
to see it from a far distance, however, through mist and rain
and darkness, we may be aware of no more than the faintest
trace of its silhouette. Then as we plod along and the weather
clears, the mountain seems clearer, it seems to grow. When
we reach its base, it seems too close, too vast, too overwhelm-
ing to see whole; yet it becomes better known as we ascend
it, and finally one dazzling day we reach the summit. So we
know ourselves, we conquer ourselves. So God, the God-
nature, is always there. It is commonplace awareness which
is far away, lost in the dark storms of our egocentric minds.

4. ON DESTINY

Man is beginning to emerge as a powerful new factor in
the universe; yet he has scarcely begun the task of transmuting personal desires into social good will, much less God's
will. But our being and our becoming are in him—this new-

comer to an obscure little planet lost in one of the millions of island universes—because beyond his grief we hear his laughter, beyond his meanness we glimpse his nobility, beyond his failures we believe in his triumphs; and because his sense of a strange and beautiful destiny is great within the soul of each of us. It is his fulfillment we work for, his distant tomorrow we serve; in order that some day, before his Father, he may know himself the worthy son of God.

5. SOME VERY SMALL PRAYERS

O God on high,
look low; and help
not only Thy saints
but Thy more abundant
sinners.

Teach me to know this, O Lord!
No matter what else I may do,
whenever I fail to love I am wrong.

Grant that I may die
in the starkest, most painful truth
than deign to live
in the happiest, most deluded ignorance.

Teach me that there will always be fools
who expect perfection from other fools.

Let me give Thee my best
that Thou may forgive my worst.

If I might learn less, my Master,
in the way a man seems to have to learn,
in the dry tears of a secret grief . . .

Teach my heartbeat to say:
I radiate Thy love
to everyone I meet:
may others find Thee through
Thy radiant love in me.

If we might thank Thee,
in spite of our disappointments,
for Thyself . . . and ask Thee,
Bless our foolish lovely earth . . .

6. WHERE LOVE IS

Late one afternoon in Kalimpong, I entered a mosque to share the evening prayer hour with Allah, and it seemed to me God was there. Then I walked by a Hindu temple to contemplate Brahman with one of his priests, and it seemed to me God was there. I sat with the lamas in their shrine room to search for the inner reality the Buddha found, and it seemed to me God was there. Then I knelt beside the church altar before its golden cross, with love seeking Him whose love seeks us, and it seemed to me God was there. I went outside and stood on the mountain. I looked at the lights in the valley. I looked at the lights in the sky. I waited. I listened. I looked at the mosque, the temple, the lamasery, the church, and I thought of all the distortions of God in time and space. And at last, while I waited, I heard a simple thing in my soul: a sigh. It was a sigh for you, for me, for all humanity, for all who have ever attempted to define Him, to limit His limitlessness. It was a sigh that said His Life is in everything and that He may be found anywhere. And it said that wherever He is sought with love by anyone at all, whether in the mosque, in the temple, in the lamasery, in the church, that always, where love is, He is there.

7. THE WORLD DISCIPLE

Now, whether you must break down barriers with your will or melt them away with your love, resolve to identify yourself with the whole of humanity, to develop a world sense, to become a world disciple. Let there no longer stand, in your consciousness, walls between nations, races, and religions; instead envision the underlying unity of all these in spiritual brotherhood. See every man as a brother and not as a citizen of a certain country, of a certain race, of a certain faith; and then see all units of humanity as individualized areas of being in the One Life. And recognize yourself not as a lone worker, but as integrated into the large and growing group of world servers, united with those who, in full spiritual consciousness, are working to fix ever more firmly the evidence of God's will being done on earth. Let your nation be the kingdom of God; let your race be the sons of God; and let your religion be the direct realization of God Himself.

8. BE LOVE

In the image of God, Man; in the image of Man, men; in the image of men, you—a seed of God-light endowed with enough power to break and remake the world.

And the power is love.

O seed of light, be blaze, be blossom, be burning star of love in the loveless human night!

CPSIA information can be obtained
at www.ICGtesting.com
Printed in the USA
LVHW081408160719
624270LV00032B/490/P